COMPLETE

AZ

Psychology

Coursework

HANDBOOK

COMPLETE
A-Z

Psychology
Coursework

HANDBOOK

Mike Cardwell
Hugh Coolican

2nd edition

Hodder & Stoughton

A MEMBER OF THE HODDER HEADLINE GROUP

Orders: please contact Bookpoint Ltd, 130 Milton Park, Abingdon, Oxon OX14 4SB. Telephone: (44) 01235 827720, Fax: (44) 01235 400454. Lines are open from 9.00–6.00, Monday to Saturday, with a 24 hour message answering service.

British Library Cataloguing in Publication Data
A catalogue record for this title is available from the British Library

ISBN 0 340 87260 8

First published 2001
Second edition 2003

Impression number   10 9 8 7 6 5 4 3 2

Year   2007 2006 2005 2004 2003

Cover photograph: C.Javier Pierini/Corbis

Typeset by Phoenix Photosetting, Chatham
and GreenGate Publishing Services, Tonbridge

Printed in Great Britain for Hodder and Stoughton Educational, a division of Hodder Headline, 338 Euston Road, London NW1 3BH, by Cox and Wyman Ltd.

Contents

Acknowledgements

The authors would like to thank AQA, Edexcel and OCR for allowing us to use coursework guidance in Chapters 12–15 and Collins Educational for permission to use the coursework checklist on pages 230–233. We would also like to thank Rob McIlveen and Alison Wadely for original suggestions for some of the studies used in Chapter 17. Finally we should acknowledge the enthusiam and endeavour of all the students who carry out coursework as part of their Psychology A level. We hope that you find this book helpful.

How to use this book

The coursework option of your psychology specification may fill you with the excitement of being a real researcher; on the other hand, it may fill you with dread because you feel out of your depth and lost for ideas. The aim of this book is to help you whatever your state of mind concerning this important part of your course. Coursework could be, and indeed should be, fun. We would like you to read this book with that, however implausible it may seem right now, firmly in mind.

Those who develop psychology specifications such as the one you are following, and indeed psychologists in general, have always emphasised the importance of coursework at A level and beyond. Psychology is, after all, based firmly on research and for many, research is what the subject is really about.

You may be content to explore the effects of different orientations of the Müller–Lyer illusion, or how long it takes people to solve anagrams, but then again you may want to use this opportunity to do something a little more significant. This book will help you every step of the way, from deciding on a research focus for your coursework right through to the final polished report.

This book has four main sections:

1   **A step-by-step approach which deals with all the different stages of the coursework process, including guidance on choosing the right area to study, deciding on your research aims and hypotheses, through design decisions, data collection and analysis, and finally writing up the finished report.**

2   **Detailed information about the specific coursework requirements of all four A level psychology specifications (AQA-A, AQA-B, Edexcel and OCR), including a breakdown of the explicit marking criteria for each section of your report.**

3   **Suggestions for coursework if you fancy something a little different. Five studies that give you some idea of the varied interests of research psychologists, and in three cases take you nowhere near real people!**

4   Valuable support material, including advice on using IT in your
     coursework, an A–Z glossary of coursework-related terms, useful
     websites, advice on ethical issues and how to deal with them, and a
     set of statistical tables. (Where these tables are referred to in the text,
     they are preceded by 'A', i.e. Table A4, etc.).

No matter how helpful books such as this may be, coursework may still
appear daunting. However, one important fact should be emphasised.
Psychology coursework has always provided students with an excellent
opportunity to improve their grades so should be taken very seriously.
Unlike the examinations that you will take at the end of your course,
coursework is entirely under your control. You choose the topic to explore,
you carry out the investigation itself, and you write up the report. Compare
that with the potential pitfalls of an unseen examination. However, you can
easily spend a long time on coursework only to see your efforts poorly
rewarded in the final mark. The primary aim of this book, therefore, is to
guide you through your psychology coursework in a manner most likely to
capitalise on your enthusiasm and so maximise the rewards you surely
deserve.

Mike Cardwell and Hugh Coolican

How to get started

Faced with a bewildering number of possibilities for your coursework, it may seem an impossible task to pick just one. It really shouldn't be that difficult – the following pointers may help narrow down your choices.

Will it be interesting (and fun)?

There is no point in carrying out research in an area that you find boring or unstimulating. One thing that characterises all researchers is the absolute enthusiasm they have for their chosen field of research. If you are really interested in the social behaviour of chimpanzees or the effects on concentration of listening to loud rock music, then it may well be possible to construct a piece of research around your interests. Chapter 17 contains a number of suggestions for studies that are interesting and fun to carry out. After all, let's not underestimate the importance of fun in all this. Your coursework isn't meant to be dull, you are actually allowed to enjoy it!

Will it be possible?

Be aware that some research is simply not possible with the time and resources available. A student of mine a few years ago announced that his A level psychology project was going to involve selective breeding among cats. His intention was to breed several generations of cats in order to see if feline intelligence could be passed from generation to generation! Needless to say, that particular piece of research never got off the ground. Some projects are far too ambitious or needlessly expensive for this level of research. The moral here is to keep it simple, unless you have the resources of a major university psychology department behind you, a team of willing and highly trained assistants, and about five years to complete your research project.

Look at other research

Reading other research, particularly published research, may well give you ideas about how you might extend a particular study, or simplify it in some way for your own research. This also helps you to find out whether there is sufficient background for your study, or whether you are going to be scrambling around desperately looking for suitable information for your introduction section. The next chapter shows you how to explore a particular topic through a variety of different avenues. A simple approach is to go to an internet search engine such as Google (www.google.com) and enter the words 'research' and 'effects of loud rock music' (or whatever) and see what comes up. You may be disappointed, or you may be pleasantly surprised. Do remember, however, that not everything you find will be the product of genuine research. You will need to sift carefully to sort the gems from the rubbish.

Have a clear aim to your research

Too often students know they want to do 'something about ...', but can't really formulate this into more concrete aims (see Chapter 4). It helps you to plan your research more effectively if you know exactly what you are trying to find out rather than just knowing you want to study a particular area. This may appear straightforward, but it is often a considerable early hurdle that students struggle to clear.

Think ahead

If you are following the AQA (A) specification, you will face questions in Unit 5 (the 'Approaches' section) that test your ability to explain a particular issue or problem. You will also be asked to explain how different perspectives could be used to research the issue or problem. It is, therefore, useful to look around at issues in your own life or in the media and think how you might both explain and explore these. You may find that one of these problems captures your imagination and becomes worthy of further research.

Ethical concerns

Given the nature of psychology, your research may well bring you into contact with members of the public. These may be people who are especially vulnerable – children, for example, so it is vital that you follow all the ethical guidelines outlined on pages 222–229 of this book. There are many ways in which participation in a study can harm or offend, and these are not always immediately obvious when planning a study. Pages 222–229 also list a number of issues that may arise when planning your research. If your intended study includes any of these issues, talk it over with your teacher before going any further.

A B C D E F G H I J K L M N O P Q R S T U V W X Y Z

How to decide on a research focus

During your course in psychology you will have to think about and come up with a specific plan for a research study; that is, you will have to decide what you are going to focus on in your coursework investigation. There is one golden rule to help you decide:

your research must be psychological.

This might sound obvious but what is meant is that your study must be based on psychological concepts and it must use psychological research methods. It must be related to prior valid research studies or published arguments in psychology. In reading your report it must be obvious that you have studied psychology and that you understand the conventional methods with which psychologists research human behaviour. Your study must differ from the sort of investigation that might be conducted by a journalist who has not studied and does not use psychology. It must look like work for psychology and not general studies.

What psychological researchers do

You are not expected to possess the expertise of a psychological researcher but let's just look at how psychological research topics are generally produced. Psychological researchers usually generate their research questions by studying current research articles in their specific interest area. They look for questions that have not been answered or aspects that need further clarification or extension. For instance, suppose it has been shown that drinking coffee appears to have the effect of improving performance on an anagram-solving task. This result might be taken as support for the theory that caffeine is an effective stimulator of word recall. Further research might involve using pure tablet-form caffeine as well as coffee, an uncaffeinated hot drink, a 'placebo' tablet (one which has no caffeine or stimulating agent) and a control group who receive nothing at all. This new research design has the power to tell us whether it is the caffeine as such which enhances performance or whether the effect is caused by the taking of a hot drink alone, the psychological knowledge that one has taken a chemical substance (the role of the placebo) or possibly a combination of these factors.

Not all psychological research is stimulated by attempts to address weaknesses in previous research. New research results from consideration of developing theory or weaknesses in previous theory. For instance, the classic 'Levels of Processing' research design was produced by researchers who wanted to show that the more meaning stimulus material has for those receiving it, the better able are they to recall that material later on. This challenged existing theory holding that it was mainly the amount of rehearsal that material received that determined its likelihood of recall.

Other new research steps out into quite uncharted territory. As a consequence of the debate generated when the US public was horrified by the well-publicised murder of Kitty Genovese, psychologists started to investigate in a hitherto relatively un-researched area – the factors which inhibit or facilitate one person's impulse to help another who is in danger or distress.

What can I do then?

As a student you will not be in a position to launch into an entirely new area such as this, nor are you likely to come up with a brilliant innovation which furthers or clarifies previous academic research. This is not what is expected. The requirement for your coursework is that you identify a research question, then set out to design a very simple research study which will address this question. You will do this by gathering data in a systematic and objective manner and conducting an analysis of this information to find the extent to which it supports your original hypothesis or aim (see page 21).

Your practical investigation must be related to subject material in the psychology syllabus that you are studying. Typically there are two major paths to developing your research project's focus, one from within and one from outside your psychology syllabus reading.

1   **Developing a research question from within your syllabus**
    Your reading in psychology might prompt you to take an existing study and attempt to replicate it in your own local environment – see Research in Practice 2. Alternatively, you might find an interesting study that suggests possible extensions. For instance, published research shows that when males are asked to estimate their own IQ, their mean estimate tends to be higher than that for females asked the

same thing. You could extend this study by comparing self-estimates of IQ with people's score on a verbal reasoning test. Do those who estimate higher IQs in fact do better on the test? This kind of study, replication or extension, is relatively easy to embed within the research literature since you have developed the research question straight from it.

2   Developing a research question from outside the syllabus
Project aims and hypotheses developed from real-life experiences are generally more intrinsically interesting and fulfilling. However, they are also danger areas in terms of ensuring that you meet all the requirements for assessment in your final project report. You must make sure that you will be able to embed your ideas in appropriate psychological content from your syllabus. In many cases, where students have tested out an interesting idea concerning human behaviour, the Introduction to their report makes it obvious that they have found it extremely difficult to find literature to support their own ideas. This is not to say that students can't have interesting and valid new ideas. The point is that the project is not intended to assess your ability to test anything; it assesses your ability to generate hypotheses and a valid research design from psychological literature and your learning experience. It is no use testing, for instance, whether girls like your favourite pop band more than boys do unless you can start with a rationale (see below) which predicts or at least suggests a difference based on psychological theory and research. This may be possible in terms of, say, self-identity, stereotyping or cognitive dissonance if the band has a strong popular 'message' (e.g. 'girl power'). However, the point is that the rationale developed from psychological theory must not appear artificially 'pasted on' to what you went ahead and tested without thinking or checking.

Having said this, it is perfectly possible to develop a testable idea from normal life experience and then to develop the appropriate psychological background to support a hypothesis. Have a look at Research in Practice 14, page 28, where Judy has been attracted by a real-life phenomenon (colourful aeroplane tail-fins) but has linked this quite sensibly with theory and research from her psychology syllabus.

Research in Practice 1

Laura read of an interesting field experiment by Cialdini, Reno and Kallgren (1990) in which the researchers handed out a leaflet to people about to enter a path. On the path they had previously left a number of pieces of litter (either 0, 1, 2, 4, 8 or 16). The idea was to see whether more pieces of litter on the road led to a greater frequency of dropping the leaflet.

She could not replicate this study exactly as it is rather elaborate and she'd have needed permission to use a public space to drop litter. Instead she created a variation of the study by asking student volunteers to a room in her college. She handed them a packet of crisps and then asked them to complete a task which entailed putting the crisp packet down. She predicted that more students would drop the packet on the floor when there was already some litter on the ground than when there wasn't.

What is a rationale?

Your *rationale* is the cement between the research literature that you will present at the beginning of your report's Introduction and the hypothesis, stated at the end of your Introduction, that you set out to test in your Method section. It is no use starting out on your study unless and until you have a clear rationale. You need to be able to explain, at least to yourself, but preferably to your tutor, just exactly why you are testing your particular hypothesis. Students often throw into their Introduction just about all they can say about their chosen topic, for instance a three-sided essay on memory. This is not at all what is required and you will lose marks if this is what you eventually do. You must present in your introduction only literature that helps you argue towards your goal. You must present an argument that explains how a particular result from the hypothesis you are going to test will support psychological theory.

Taking Laura's proposed littering study as an example, she can discuss, very briefly, the general issues concerned with both conformity and modelling, getting on fairly swiftly to one or two studies, like the Cialdini *et al.* research, which deals with providing models in naturalistic settings to see whether these influence people's behaviour in an area where we would normally expect 'good citizen' behaviour. (There are several of these, mostly to do with the variables that prompt bystanders to help or which inhibit helping.) Her rationale will move the account from the background literature, through the Cialdini *et al.* study, to her own variation where she predicts that, based on Cialdini *et al.*'s findings, she would expect more crisp packet dropping in the condition where there are already some packets lying on the floor.

Points to consider when settling on a research focus
CHOOSE A CLEAR AND LIMITED CONTEXT

Students very often focus on a vast area of possible research. In other words they have not focused much at all. For instance, a popular but quite unrealistic starting point is to be 'interested in what makes people creative'. This is not a focus. It is a vast area for academic research and debate. You will not be able to determine the causes of any psychological characteristic. Psychologists have never isolated such causes, there are always many and varied factors at work and the concept of 'creativity' itself is multi-faceted and much debated.

However, a certain amount of reading about creativity will teach you that there are ways to assess very limited areas of 'divergent thinking' ability. You might, for instance, ask people to think of unusual uses for everyday objects (such as a brick) and take as a measure the rarity of each response (how infrequently it is produced by any of your participants). You could alternatively ask a colleague to rate the responses using criteria such as how unusual and inventive they found each answer.

Your reading might generate the following two theoretical questions.

1   To what extent is creative thinking innate?

2   Is it the case that people who have become skilled in convergent thinking (finding answers through strictly logical means) tend not to be good at divergent thinking?

You cannot answer such broad questions but you can test simple hypotheses that follow *from* such broad suggestions. To support the notion that divergent thinking is innate you could correlate (see page 47) scores on your test produced by parents and their children (your student friends), not forgetting that such a correlation would also support the notion that parents pass creativity on to their children through example and teaching. On the second question you could attempt to show that maths students perform worse on your divergent exercise than arts students. You may not get the result you predict in your research (you probably won't for these two examples) but this is not the point of coursework. The idea is that you can demonstrate the ability to design and carry out a very limited piece of research which fairly and objectively tests a simple hypothesis generated by a broader theory.

BASE YOUR CONTEXT ON READING

Students have the hardest time with their coursework when they choose a topic which fascinates them, and commit themselves to it before they have done any reading. What do students find fascinating? Crime, sex, music, mental illness, love, telepathy, the environment, religion, animal rights. Open any psychology textbook and you won't find much on these topics and you'll find even less that lends itself to simple empirical research. This is not to say that the adaptive and resourceful student could not investigate any of these areas successfully. Anything is possible. However, the situation to avoid is one where you have committed yourself to a topic, perhaps even designed materials, and where you then find yourself struggling to identify literature that relates to what you intend to do or have done.

As you read through the psychology in any major textbook, and as you go through work in class, you should find that, every so often, you can pause and ask 'Hmm could I do something like that?'. Very often you could, with some adaptation of the original design to your circumstances. It is best to make a note in a diary page when something interests you and to come back to the list you have made when the time comes to choose a topic.

TRY DIFFERENT SOURCES FOR A FOCUS

There are various sources from which you are likely to be able to find a research project that you can undertake:

* **reading psychology texts** – this was discussed above

* **your tutor** – tutors usually have a stock of 'classic' studies which you can adapt; you could also ask to look at earlier student work for inspiration (but of course you may not plagiarise)

* **practical books** – several textbooks (including this one) provide examples of practicals that you can conduct; some texts are dedicated to just this topic (e.g. *BPS Manual of Practicals*)

- **the internet** – nowadays this is a rich source; if you browse the research methods pages of university psychology websites you will very soon come across many practical ideas (there are probably sites dedicated to psychology practicals at your level which can be found with a little thoughtful searching).

- **journals** – if you are lucky enough to have access to a university library you can browse though research journals. Beware though. These tend to be set in highly scientific and technical language and to present fairly complex work. However, there are simple little gems dotted around and even a complex idea can often be simplified. Several journals are accessible in electronic form on the internet and even where these only contain titles of articles, they can often stimulate an idea for a simple project. A complex study on some incomprehensible aspect of linguistic structure carried out on children in several countries might prompt you to realise that you could compare Hindi and non-Hindi speaking English children on learning new foreign language words.

THINK OF ETHICS BEFORE YOU FOCUS

Some areas of research are ethical no-go areas. You may find yourself fascinated by mental health, eating disorders, physical abuse of children, criminality and so on. However, you are not going to be able to study these areas directly. The only thing you might be able to do is to study people's attitude to the issues involved. For instance, you can find out what people think about physical punishment or you can assess the knowledge of different groups of people about what constitutes or might cause an eating disorder.

ESTABLISHING A THEORETICAL AND/OR RESEARCH CONTEXT

Before you finally settle on the area and questions that your project is going to tackle you need to make sure that you will be able to justify your hypotheses in the light of psychological theory and prior research. This is the purpose of the 'rationale' that we discussed on page 7.

If your project question comes from your reading in psychology then there should not be too great a problem in establishing the background theory and research. You will have already come across it in order to decide upon your adaptation or extension of it. However, even where your study is a version of one you have read, or is a simple extension of it, you will need to be sure that you can get your hands on enough literature to provide a sound start to your study. Sometimes you might find an interesting study but little else in the textbook you are reading, upon which to base your 'Introduction'.

If you have developed your research question from outside the syllabus (see page 6) then this phase of your project is crucial. We said earlier that it is no use getting quite a long way with your research only to find that the question is interesting but that it does not relate easily to psychological theory or that what literature there is exists in very obscure corners.

How do I find literature relevant to my chosen topic?

The answers here are going to be similar to those given above to the question of where to look for a focus. The difference here is that you have now decided, provisionally, on a focus but are looking for theory to back up, or to add further context to, what you have chosen to do. Here are some directions you can take.

1   Library
   If you are lucky enough to have access to a good academic library (your own college or a nearby university) then you need to browse through this, usually not only tackling the general textbook section but also consulting the catalogue (which normally uses Dewey decimal numbers) to find more specific texts in the area of your study. When you browse be sure to make good, thoughtful use of the rear index. You may not find 'audience effects', for instance, but you might find something under 'social facilitation'. You may not find 'racism' but you may well find 'prejudice', 'stereotyping' or 'ethnicity' and 'attitude'. Ask your tutor for the likely alternative terms in your chosen area.

2   Electronic abstracts
   There are several sets of CD discs (e.g. *Psychlit* and *Psychinfo*) which you can browse in an academic library or on the internet if your institution has paid for a licence. These provide an abstract of the main features of virtually all studies published in psychology. You need to be very careful when searching these as each has its own search 'language'. For instance, if you enter 'sex-role socialisation' the programme will only return those articles which mention these two terms specifically together. It will not find, for instance, 'sex-role development'. You need to enter 'sex-role' and 'socialisation' separately and also see what you get when these are combined. If this

11

doesn't produce much then try taking out 'socialisation' and putting in 'development' and so on. These sources will throw up many journal articles that you are not likely to be able to get hold of. However, on the one hand you might obtain enough information just from the abstract, and on the other hand, some of the articles might be worth obtaining through your library or tutor.

3   Internet
    The internet is an extremely rich source of information. You will be able to access abstracts, as above, or the main contents of articles by going to the sites of electronic journals, or you can find all sorts of psychology-related sites within universities and colleges where you can access the information you need to provide a theoretical background to your research question. However you should be very careful when using internet source material. Make sure it is from a genuine and recognised academic source. It is no use citing material that you obtained from 'Charlie's Psych Psyte'. You have no way of knowing whether the material is completely invented or entirely false.

PULLING THE CONTEXT TOGETHER

Don't use anything and everything you find that is somehow related to your topic. Much of the material you read whilst reviewing literature may be irrelevant. Don't feel that you simply must include everything you find. As you prepare material for your 'Introduction' (see page 101) be parsimonious – use only what is directly relevant and that which will bring your argument, through the rationale, neatly and concisely to your hypotheses.

Research in Practice 2
Establishing a research and theory context

Kelly decided to conduct a study which would support the theory that working with others has the effect of inhibiting task performance. She had participated in a similar experiment in her first year at college and found the topic fascinating. She had also picked up some major topics within this area from her lectures in social psychology. She knew she would have two conditions – one where a participant performed a task alone and another where the task was observed. She looked up the topic in Gross (*Psychology: The Science of Mind and Behaviour*, London: Hodder and Stoughton, 1996). This provided her with several perspectives on the general idea of action in the presence of others. First there were studies on direct competition with others. Second, there was the situation where one is observed by others and the idea that evaluation by others is a factor which affects performance. Finally there was the suggestion that the mere presence of others affects performance (whether they evaluate one's performance or not). Although it contained the important arguments, Gross did not provide her with background research on the 'mere presence' hypothesis so, armed with her lecture notes, she went to the college library and checked a couple of general psychology textbooks. In the rear indexes she had to look up 'social facilitation', 'audience effects', 'social influence' and, in one case, only 'social loafing' in order to find the exact location of relevant theory and research. She discovered a study which had tried to distinguish between the effects of evaluation and 'mere presence' performance of a task compared with doing that task when completely alone. The conditions were: performing a task (a) with the experimenter watching (evaluation), (b) alone, and (c) with 'another participant' present who was 'waiting for a different experiment' ('mere presence' condition).

Kelly also had to decide whether to use a simple or a complex task, since all the texts discussed research showing that people tend to do better on a simple task in front of an audience but worse on more complex tasks. She thought that most of the complex tasks described might take too long and were too vulnerable to other variables (such as the educational experience of participants) to show an effect in the limited conditions in which she would perform her experiment.

She decided therefore to use a simple task and to use an 'alone' condition and a 'presence' condition where an 'electrician' (a class colleague) would be present in the room with the participant 'fixing a fuse'. Hence, in this condition, there should be no evaluation effect on the task but there would be a person present while it was being

Continued

completed. If 'mere presence' affects performance it should do so here. In order to obtain more background on her particular study, as now planned, she asked the library to get hold of a copy of the original 'mere presence' article through the inter-Library loan system. She found that she had to pay a small fee for this service but the article arrived promptly just ten days later, as it was published in a prestigious and well-used psychological research journal. While she was waiting for the research article she also consulted some social psychology textbooks in her library and on a one-day visit to her local university library which was arranged after a quick phone call from her tutor. She gathered quite a lot more material from these texts but began to realise that she was accumulating notes which ranged either too far from her topic or went too deeply into theory for her to be able to use all of it in her Introduction. She began to sift through and pull out only that which was either directly relevant to her argument for 'mere presence' or which could serve as a brief introduction to the topic of social facilitation in general.

CHANGING YOUR FOCUS OR TOPIC

Don't feel, once you have stated your intended project title, that you must remain committed to exactly that topic. Things change as you review literature and think about designs. For instance, Kelly discovered that the nature of the task, whether it was simple or complex, had a bearing on expected results so she had to consider this while designing her study. Some designs may turn out to be unworkable. Some topics may generate too little available psychological background, or even too much. You may find that what you proposed in fact turns out to be too vast a topic area for a simple research project. You may find that there are more interesting hypotheses to be tested than those you originally thought of.

This is fine and part of the learning process. However, of course you should not leap about from topic to topic as the weeks go by just because your tutor has covered some more interesting area or because you keep finding the grass greener in the other chapters of your textbook. If you change your topic too late you may well find that you have left too little time for a thorough literature review, for development of sound resources and for testing enough participants.

There are always more interesting topic areas but you cannot afford to flit about. It is probably safer to stick with what initially interested you. It will probably interest you again once your results are in. If you are continuing with psychology you can always use the newer topics you find in later projects at A level or beyond.

A B C D E F G H I J K L M N O P Q R S T U V W X Y Z

The project brief

Students who are following the AQA (A) specification are required to produce a project brief before starting any data collection. This has two functions.

- **It helps your teacher check that your study is realistically planned and does not break any ethical guidelines.**

- **It enables you to include the sort of material that would not usually be found in a journal article (such as the advantages and disadvantages of the methods used etc.) and also means that this material does not have to be included in the report itself. This makes your actual report far closer to the type of report that those of you who go on to study psychology at university would be required to produce.**

Research in Practice 3

Derry had read that as boys and girls grow, their parents begin to give them tasks that either take them out into the world (thus encouraging independence) or keep them in the home (thus encouraging dependence). She had noted that boys tend to be given tasks that take them out into the world (e.g. taking the rubbish out) whereas girls are often given tasks that keep them closer to the parent (e.g. assisting with domestic chores). Derry approached a local post-natal clinic and asked if she could observe how parents typically interact with their babies when they brought them in for their regular check-ups. She was particularly interested in whether there was a gender difference in the way boys and girls were held by the mother. If this 'inside-outside' bias for boys and girls began very early, she expected to find that boys would be held facing away from the mother and girls held facing towards the mother.

In your *project brief*, you should answer the following questions:

1 **Identify the aim of the research and state the experimental/ alternative and null hypothesis** (There are no marks awarded for this – they will be credited in the report itself)

Research in Practice 4

The aim of this research is to investigate whether there are perspective differences in the way that mothers hold their male and female babies (the **aim**).

It is hypothesised that when mothers hold their babies on their knees, there is a difference in the inwards or outwards facing perspective offered to boys and girls (the **alternative hypothesis**).

There is no difference in the way that mothers hold their male and female babies. Girls are as likely to be held with an outward facing perspective as are boys (the **null hypothesis**).

2 **Explain why a directional or a non-directional experimental/ alternative hypothesis has been selected**   (1 mark)

Research in Practice 5

A non-directional hypothesis is chosen. Research shows gender differences in the way parents treat boys and girls with respect to activities that either take them out of the home or keep them in it. However, there is no evidence that this difference extends to the perspective offered to young babies when being held by their parents.

3 **Identify the chosen research method [laboratory experiment, field experiment, natural experiment, survey, observation or correlational research] and [if appropriate] the research design chosen**   (1 mark)

Research in Practice 6

This is a naturalistic observation.

4 **Evaluate the advantages and disadvantages of the chosen research method**   (2 marks)

A B C D E F G H I J K L M N O P Q R S T U V W X Y Z

Research in Practice 7

The major advantage of this method is its ability to explore behaviour in its natural setting without the constraints of laboratory or experimental artificiality.

However, if participants become aware of the observer's presence, their behaviour becomes less natural because of their reaction to an extra feature of the situation, the presence of an observer.

5   Identify potential sources of bias in the investigation and any possible confounding variables   (2 marks)

Research in Practice 8

It is possible that mothers may react to my presence and respond differently. The presence of a stranger without a baby in the post-natal clinic may be treated with some suspicion and distract mothers so that their behaviour is not natural. It is also possible that mothers adopt a different position for their baby depending on whether they expect their baby to empty its bladder once undressed. Facing the baby outwards may minimise the damage to the parent!

6   Explain what procedures will be adopted to deal with these   (2 marks)

Research in Practice 9

In order to make my observations as natural and unobtrusive as possible, I intend to visit the post-natal clinic regularly for a period of two months prior to the study. In this way, mothers will get used to my presence and treat me as if I was a student on work experience. It is difficult to know how to deal with the latter problem. However, I will interview each mother afterwards, asking them whether such considerations were a part of their decision to position their child the way that they did. This will also give me the opportunity to offer some debriefing.

7 **Select an appropriate level of statistical significance to be reached before the hypothesis will be retained** (1 mark)

Research in Practice 10

$p \leq 0.05$

8 **Identify any relevant ethical considerations and explain the steps to be taken to deal with these** (3 marks)

Research in Practice 11

No informed consent can be obtained but participants are being observed in a public place where they know they are being watched anyway (e.g. by other mothers and by the nursing staff) so this is not regarded as being a difficult ethical problem. It is important to maintain anonymity of all participants, therefore no names or other identifying features of the participants will be used in the report.

Setting your aims and hypotheses

What is the aim of a study?

The aim of a study is, broadly speaking, what it is intended to show, establish or do. In psychology the aim of a study is very often to support or challenge a theory by testing hypotheses which are generated from it – see Research in Practice 12.

Research in Practice 12
Hypotheses in Kelly's 'mere presence' study

Kelly constructed her study as a two-condition experiment in which participants either performed a peg-board task in a quiet room, alone (they had to move pegs as quickly as possible from one set of positions to another) or in a room where an 'electrician was fixing a fuse' (the electrician being a colleague). This study was intended to support the theory that the mere presence of others has the effect of inhibiting task performance.

She hypothesised that people perform a peg-board task faster in the presence of others, since this is a simple task and prior research suggests facilitation of simple tasks with an audience. She found that participants in the 'presence' condition did perform the task more quickly (her statistical test showed significance – see page 80). Therefore she had support for her hypothesis and for the theory in general. The result did not *prove* that people perform faster in the presence of others. There are several other possible explanations of the effect (such as that the 'presence' group were just better peg placers).

You are very likely to carry out such a study for your coursework. However, some psychological studies are more descriptive. They might have the aims of:

- **finding out how people generally discipline their children**
- **measuring current attitudes to capital punishment**
- **observing typical two-person interactions in a children's playground**
- **using a new reading ability scale to gather data on a large sample of the population**
- **developing a reliable and valid scale to measure certain aspects of personality.**

Check your syllabus requirements before settling on the final aims and design of your study, to see whether you must test a hypothesis or whether it is permitted to conduct a descriptive study of the kind indicated just above. Note that the last two in this list are well beyond the scope of a basic level psychology practical assignment.

What is a hypothesis?

A hypothesis is a claim about the world. It is a statement of what you believe to be true and it usually occurs in the process of trying to outline what should be the case if a theory is to be supported. However, there is a tendency in research writing to use the term hypothesis for another purpose and that is to make a prediction. Kelly predicted that her sample performing a task in the presence of another would be take less time than would the sample performing alone.

Kelly's *hypothesis* was:

people perform the peg-board task faster in the presence of another than when alone.

Kelly's *research prediction* was: (often called the 'research hypothesis')

my sample of participants performing in the presence of another will perform faster than those working alone.

In statistical tests of significance we assume that the sample of people we test are a representative sample of the population about whom we make a hypothesis. *Hypotheses are about populations.* To test our hypothesis we first assume that there is no difference between the populations from which the samples were taken. This is known as the null hypothesis (H_0) and would be written here formally as:

The mean time for peg-board completion in the presence of another is equal to the mean time for peg-board completion when alone.

We make this assumption, then calculate the probability that our two samples would differ as they did if this were true. If this probability comes out as very low (lower than 0.05) then we reject the null hypothesis and accept, provisionally, the alternative hypothesis (H_1). This is the hypothesis we wish to support and is written formally as:

The mean time for peg-board completion in the presence of another is lower than the mean time for peg-board completion when alone.

The research hypothesis is often called the 'alternative hypothesis' though strictly speaking the alternative and null hypotheses are always statistical statements about populations. What are called research hypotheses are usually predictions about what is expected to happen with the samples in the present study.

There are three important implications here for your study.

1   **You must state your research prediction clearly in your report so you must be extremely clear about this before you start gathering your data.**

2   **Never try to 'prove' or support the null hypothesis. Don't run a study where you want to show there is *no* difference between conditions or groups. Significance testing works on the principle of estimating whether a found difference between samples is likely to represent a real difference between underlying populations or not. It is quite a different matter to try to demonstrate that a small difference between samples is evidence that there is *no* difference between underlying populations.**

3   **You must be clear about what variables are to be measured in your study and how. It is this that will drive the design of your study, so you cannot go any further until hypotheses are clearly stated and variables are operationally defined.**

Operational definitions

An operational definition is a specification of exactly how a variable will be measured. 'Task performance' in the 'mere presence' study above was operationally defined as time (in seconds) taken to complete a peg-board task. 'Memory' needs to be defined in terms of the task set – for instance, number of words correctly recalled from a list in three minutes. General aspects of behaviour like 'confidence' or even 'aggression' are usually quite hard to define. However, you must create suitable operational definitions before you can even think about data gathering for your project.

If your measures are inappropriate or loosely organised then you cannot be sure that you have really shown what you intended to show in a research study. For instance, suppose students attempted to measure altruism using the item below.

> You are walking to work one day and you see a man lying on the pavement.

On the scale below mark how likely you would be to help the man:

Very likely	Rather likely	Unsure	Rather unlikely	Very unlikely

The trouble with this measure is that it could be assessing a lot of things other than simple desire or tendency to help. Suppose the participant asked is female? Would they be likely to help a man in a quiet back street? Suppose the area is one where drunks often lie on the pavement? The person asked might be a single parent who always has to hurry to work after seeing their children to school. They might be just as altruistic as the next person but they just dare not lose their job.

A better measure of altruism here might be a questionnaire or scale (see page 52) which uses several items like the one above in order to ask about helping tendencies in a variety of contexts, not just one.

Research in Practice 13

Tutor: So what hypothesis have you decided to test, Vijay?

Vijay: Well we reckon people will be more courteous to a smartly dressed person who holds open a door than to a scruffy person.

Tutor: And how exactly do you propose to test that hypothesis then?

Vijay: We're going to sit in the college foyer and observe what people do when Nick holds the door open for them.

A B C D E F G H I J K L M N O P Q R S T U V W X Y Z

Continued

One day he'll be smartly dressed and the other day he'll dress scruffily.

Tutor: OK ... so what are the main variables in this study then?

Vijay: Well, one is the variable of dressing – smart and scruffy.

Tutor: Yes, and the other?

Vijay: Courtesy. We're observing courteous behaviour.

Tutor: ... and exactly how will you measure that then?

Vijay: We... we... well...er... we... look at how courteous they are.

Tutor: Yes but how will you assess that one person is more courteous than another?

Vijay: Well, we'll go by what they say, whether they say thank you or not, and... face... we'll look at their face and see if they smile or look positively at Nick... er and that sort of thing.

Tutor: Hmm you really need to go away and come back with a clearer definition of what you're going to count as 'courteous' behaviour don't you?

Vijay: Right...

This sort of conversation between tutor and student preparing a practical exercise is exceedingly common. Very often it is quite easy to drum up the structure of a study which will, in principle, test the hypothesis you have decided to investigate. It often involves looking for a difference between two sorts of people or across two experimental conditions that are relatively simple to define. However, when it comes to the measure of behaviour to be observed (the dependent variable in an experiment – see page 37) life becomes exceedingly difficult for the novice psychological researcher and indeed is one of the greatest areas of difficulty. It is even difficult for seasoned psychologists who have spent decades developing subtle behavioural measures, so you're hardly likely to find ways to measure behaviour unambiguously without a struggle.

The most important things to remember when seeking a manageable measure of behaviour are shown in the following table.

Table 1 How to seek a manageable measure of behaviour

Keep it simple	e.g. Does a driver stop or not? Do people smile or not?
Make sure others could easily measure as you did	The measures you use must be clearly defined in your report. For instance, not 'we gave a score from 1 to 10 based on how aggressive the action was' but 'we scored each act for aggression according to the observation checklist below' (see page 66).
Set a realistic task	Do not ask people to recall a list of 50 or more items. Do not give a numerical test that lasts an hour and contains really difficult problems. If testing children, in particular, do trial runs to see what the proposed age of child can in fact do.
Make sure questions, if used, are simple, clear and unambiguous	See pages 56–58.
Use an existing psychological scale	Some psychological scales are freely available for use (e.g. locus of control) because they are published in articles or in textbooks. However, beware of scales that just 'come your way'. These may be subject to copyright and you may infringe this if you use them. In addition, be very careful about ethical and sensitive issues. Students are not qualified psychologists and would be extremely ill-advised to use a scale which assesses a clinical condition such as depression, for instance.
Develop a scale	Where there is time and sufficient support teaching, students can develop their own scale, especially those measuring attitudes. See page 53.
Decide on your type of measure	e.g. whether you want to use a categorical or a measured variable. See below.
Think carefully about the implications of the type of measure you have chosen	See the discussion below.

We will now look more closely at the ways in which variables can be defined and measured.

VARIABLES

These are anything in the world that can change and therefore take differing values. For instance temperature is a variable about whose changes we are usually all too well aware. Note that 'heat' is a general term referring to what we can feel when the weather becomes warmer. However, 'temperature' can be defined as an operational measure of heat. That is, we can say exactly how it will be measured (e.g. by the expansion of mercury) and in what units.

Categorical variables

Categorical variables are ones where differences between people are identified only by categories, not by measurements along some kind of scale. For instance we often separate people according to occupation: nurse, doctor, teacher, receptionist and so on. Other examples might be: the way people vote (Labour, Conservative, etc.), the colour of your bedroom, the area of the UK in which you live, your ethnic identity and so on. In an experiment (see page 37) the independent variable (that is, the conditions of the experiment) is usually categorical. For instance, the audience experiment described above had an independent variable with two levels – 'in the presence of another' and 'alone'. These are measures but only at a very crude level – people either perform alone or with another.

Measured variables – interval and ordinal level scales

Other variables are measured at a more sophisticated level. Often the distinction is made between *categorical variables* (like those just mentioned above) and *measured variables*. Temperature is a measured variable. We can say that 40° is a certain amount hotter than 20° and that 32° is somewhere in between. We can't do that with a categorical variable. We can't say that the occupation of nursing is somewhere in between the occupations of architect and sales assistant (though of course we can say this about the salaries for these occupations).

On an *interval scale* each category of measurement on the scale represents an equal magnitude. Hence, on a ruler each inch is exactly the same length and on a temperature scale each unit represents the same amount of change.

STANDARDISED AND NON-STANDARDISED MEASURES

Many psychological measures appear to be at an interval level. If you ask people to rate themselves on their usual level of anxiety on a scale of 0 (low) to 100 (high), you will obtain a set of values that look like an interval measure. Some people will score 80 and some as low as 15. However, there is no way you can claim that 10 points on this scale is the same 'amount' of anxiety wherever it falls. You are using a non-standardised measure of self-reported anxiety. Psychologists have invented scales to measure anxiety and these have been standardised. The process of *standardisation* is a long complicated research procedure involving testing of large samples and adjustment of items in the scale until there is a fairly even distribution of scores.

This ideal of standardisation is never perfectly achieved of course. However, as a general rule of thumb, you can assume in your psychological research work that if a scale has been standardised then we can treat the data gathered on this scale as being at interval level. Examples would be measures of anxiety on Spielberger's state/trait anxiety scale or scores on Eysenck's extroversion/introversion measure.

If the scale has not been standardised (e.g. it is your own rating scale like the one described for anxiety above) then you will be safer reducing your data to *ordinal level*. This means giving each score a rank and then using one of the non-parametric rank tests described on pages 85–89.

Level of measurement – it's partly your choice

No measurement system is natural or pre-ordained. It is humans who decide how they will measure a natural phenomenon. You should avoid asking the question 'At what level of measurement are the data?' and think in terms of 'At what level are we treating the data?' or 'At what level did we set our measures?'. We can always reduce interval to ordinal data and we can also reduce ordinal and interval data to categorical data simply by counting how many people fell into sections of the measurement scale. For instance, 30 participants' scores on a mathematical test may be reduced to a categorical variable by finding the mean and dividing the scores into two categories – above the mean and below the mean. In each cell now you will only have a frequency and you could perform a chi-square test on these (see page 82).

However you cannot increase the level of data measurement once data are in. If you originally asked people whether they believed in physical punishment or not you can't now find out how *strongly* they believed in it. This is why you must think about your measures and your proposed statistical analysis, in conjunction with your hypothesis, *before* you start data gathering.

Research in Practice 14

Judy went to the airport to meet relatives. Whilst there she noticed that some British Airways planes had very bright, attractive tails. Her mother explained that BA had changed to these brightly coloured tail-fins some years ago in an attempt to change their image and attract more customers. Judy had her A level coursework project on her mind and also recalled her teacher talking about extroversion and introversion during the previous week. In particular she remembered that extroverts were thought to seek stimulation because they had low cortical arousal. Judy proposes to assess the degree to which extroverts and introverts find the BA tail-fins attractive.

We can say the following things about Judy's proposed project.

Aim: To investigate extroverts' and introverts' liking of BA's tailfins as this relates to the biological theory of extroversion.

Theory: Judy's project will attempt to support the theory that extroverts have lower cortical arousal and therefore tend to seek stimulation whereas introverts try to avoid it.

Hypothesis (general): Extroverts find BA tail-fins more attractive than do introverts.

Research prediction (or 'research hypothesis'): A sample of extroverts will find BA tailfins more attractive than will a sample of introverts.

In order to test her hypothesis Judy has to turn it into a testable statement or claim. That is, she must provide an operationalised version of her variables and design a study which will test her hypothesis accurately and with as little ambiguity as is possible.

She has to find a sample of extroverts and introverts and measure their reaction to the tail-fins. The wording of her hypothesis makes her group variable (introvert or extrovert) a categorical variable. She can use a scale to measure a large number of people for extroversion. She

Continued

can then take the top scoring 20 per cent and call these extroverts while the lowest scoring 20 per cent are treated as introverts. Here a measured variable (degree of extroversion) has been reduced to a categorical one. She could of course leave the extroversion scores as they are and see whether higher extroversion scores are related to greater liking for the tail-fin. This is a *correlational* hypothesis and we shall discuss these on page 47. However, in her hypothesis as stated, Judy is using two categories – extrovert and introvert.

For her behaviour measure of liking Judy could simply ask each person whether they do or don't like the tail-fins, producing another categorical variable. Alternatively she could ask them to rate the tail-fins on a scale of 1 to 10. In this way her liking variable would become a measured one, best treated as ordinal.

Let's now summarise and take a look at the steps Judy took to develop her testable hypothesis:

- **find a phenomenon which relates to psychological theory x**
- **check theory for implications (see how phenomenon relates to theory and research in the psychology on your syllabus)**
- **develop a general hypothesis from theory; consider your rationale**
- **develop a specific prediction from the general hypothesis**
- **state the prediction in operationally testable terms (i.e. find ways to measure and control your variables).**

(The alternative is to find an existing study that you can repeat in your own environment or a study which follows from existing theory or research, as described on page 9.)

A B C D E F G H I J K L M N O P Q R S T U V W X Y Z

Choosing a method

Ideally speaking, the choice of method in a research project is that which is best suited to the hypothesis or research question. However, you may be constrained in your choice by the requirements of the particular examination board you are working under. What you should certainly do is to find out exactly what kinds of research design are required by that examination board. You should not end up in a position in which you are worried about whether your research design will 'count'.

You will have to consider several major questions before starting your research. These are:

* **where will the study take place?**
* **who will be studied?**
* **how will data be measured and collected?**
* **how will the measures affect the hypothesis?**

Never start on your data gathering before you have sought the advice of your tutor, otherwise you could end up with a pile of data that you cannot use, or a design which is so faulty that no conclusion is possible from the research exercise you have carried out.

Let's look at a set of suggestions made by students in Mr Ogden's practical psychology class and the recommendations he has made for them.

1   **Julie is interested in whether it really is, as it seems to her, harder to grasp information in the early morning than it is later in the day. She wants to see whether recall of facts in a piece of text will be worse at 9 a.m. than it is at 1.00 p.m.**

2   **Mark saw a programme about face recognition on the television in which it was claimed that customers, in a brief encounter, typically don't notice that a returning shop assistant is a different person to the first one, who ducked out of sight to fetch the customer's goods. They did tend to notice, however, if the assistant made a pleasant comment before disappearing below the counter.**

3   Rajinder is interested in whether children who play alone are more likely to be bullied.

4   Sheila wonders whether truck drivers will differ from students in their attitude to the environment and road transport.

5   Doug wishes to discover the ways in which people think about their environment and its preservation. That is, he is interested in existing 'schemas' or 'models' that ordinary people use in order to understand their environment.

In order to decide upon a method you must find the answers to several questions and the following are probably the most important of these:

- **where should the study take place?**
- **who should we study?**
- **how should we gather our data?**

Where to conduct the study – laboratory or field?

Julie needs to control her conditions quite carefully since the task she wants her participants to perform is one requiring concentration. She would also like to control all extraneous variables (see Chapter 6) because these could easily interfere with performance on the recall task. Therefore she could conduct her study as a laboratory experiment. For psychological research this will not be a room packed with retort stands and bubbling flasks. It need only be a quiet classroom, or even your own bedroom at home. Anywhere as long as you can:

- **keep conditions constant**
- **keep any slight distractions (e.g. the heating system noise) to a minimum.**

Jason's study would be odd in a laboratory since we require a 'natural' situation – people being served in a shop or collecting their keys from a hotel reception desk. Jason was lucky. He knew the staff in the assignment collection office and they agreed to let him and a colleague hand back assignments (under supervision) and to change places between the student asking for their work and the 'assistant' (Jason or his colleague) handing it over. For half the students, randomly selected, the assistant uttered a pleasant comment about the weather. A third colleague stopped each student outside the assignment office and asked whether they had noticed the swap.

This study still counts as an experiment – see Chapter 6 – but it is one conducted 'in the field'. Obviously variables cannot be completely controlled.

A B C D E F G H I J K L M N O P Q R S T U V W X Y Z

People can say different things, they might look in different directions, there may be a variety of distractions, noise, light changes and so on and any of these might have a serious effect on the outcomes of this experiment.

Who to study?

Rajinder cannot perform an experiment. She would find it difficult both practically and ethically to arrange for children to play alone in order to see whether they were bullied or not. She will have to study children in a natural setting. She could conceivably ask parents to bring children to her college or house in order to be questioned but this is hardly realistic. Her best approach would be to observe children in the playground, if she receives permission from a school, and to take note of who plays alone. Ethically of course she can't just stand by if she observes children being bullied. She might interview the children or ask them to complete a simple questionnaire. She might interview the teacher or she might have to record only a very mild measure of 'bullying' which involves noting the extent to which each child is on the giving or receiving end of aggressive actions.

Sheila is lucky because her father runs a garage and she can give a questionnaire to truck drivers who agree to assist her (helping her father in the garage shop and listening to drivers' conversations is partly what gave her the idea in the first place). She has to use students as a comparison group. The trouble is students differ not only in being students but also in age. Perhaps she can ask only mature students at her college and make sure she gets a roughly equivalent group.

Doug could use the 'laboratory' or a natural situation (e.g. asking people in a quiet classroom set up for interviews or in the college refectory). He could ask almost anyone but, of course, the kind of persons he picks will probably have a direct impact on the kinds of models of the environment that will emerge.

The idea of sampling

The idea of samples is that the people you select for a study are supposed to be representative of some population to which you would like to generalise your results. Think of a coffee buyer sampling coffee beans and assuming that the sample taken is representative of all the sacks to be purchased.

The best method for taking a representative sample from a population is to sample at random. This does not mean taking people as and when you can get them. This is 'haphazard' or 'opportunity sampling' (those I could get).

Random sampling is very rarely carried out by psychological researchers when they obtain participants. Most samples are composed of students or volunteers. Only large scale surveys, well resourced, can attempt to select people randomly from an identified population. Hence never say that your sample was a 'random sample' – your marker won't believe you! You use volunteers, a captive, 'opportunity' or 'convenience' sample, or you can just be honest and say that the sample comprised friends, neighbours and colleagues whom you could persuade to take part.

How many participants should I use?

The answer is like that to 'how long is a piece of string?'. The larger the sample you take, for an experiment or in a survey, then the closer will your sample statistics be to the true statistics of the underlying population. However, there are diminishing returns. If you are testing a real experimental effect (something that *does* usually 'work'), then taking 100 participants will not give you that much greater accuracy than will taking 30. However five is certainly too small. For most 'classic' psychology experiments, 15 to 20 in each group will do. For questionnaire surveys there are various formulae depending on the size of the population you wish to tap into. The problem here is that this size is rarely known and that you will only have the time and resources to test a smallish number of people. Never mind! The idea of the project is that you gain experience in research techniques, not aim to publish in a scientific journal. Obviously, test all you can but keep this reasonable – you will not want to, or perhaps be able to analyse the data from hundreds of people who have answered a 30-item questionnaire! Usually, 30 to 40 is ample. The absolutely crucial thing is to recognise the limitations of your sample both by giving specific details in the 'Participants' section of your report and also by picking up this point in your discussion. Most psychology experiments are performed on American students and psychology has a long way to go in testing out its theories across most of the rest of the world!

Make sure before you start that you will be able to get enough people into each condition of your study. You probably won't be able to find 20 left-handed firemen to test so change your project idea straight away!

Make sure that anyone you do test is cordially invited into your study and given the opportunity to give informed consent to participate (see page 224). Include a consent form in the appendices of your report (page 225).

How to gather data

Most student practicals use a quantitative approach but a growing number may be qualitative. Quantitative studies gather data by taking some measure of variables. This measure must be objective and reliable. It should be possible for someone else, taking the same measurements of the same events, to come up with almost exactly the same values. Let's think about the sorts of measures that the students above could employ.

1   Julie's task looks easy enough. She has to count how many facts each participant correctly recalls from the text they have received earlier. However, she must be careful to specify, in advance if possible, what will count and what will not. For instance, would 'The man found a new home' be counted as a correct recall of 'The man bought a new house'? We might award half marks for cases like this or we might be very strict and only accept perfect wording. The important criterion is that Julie chooses a scoring method and uses this consistently. If not she could be accused of making the scoring process suit her hypothesis.

2   Jason has to find a measure that will accurately record whether the person did in fact notice the change of assistant. Leading questions are a problem. Asking 'Did you notice that the assistant changed?' could well prompt answers that begin with 'Now you come to mention it ...'. Again there will be the possibility of recording half marks but otherwise each participant will be recorded as either a 'yes' or a 'no' – a categorical variable.

3   Rajinder's task is quite difficult. Reliable and accurate observations of freely occurring behaviour are notoriously difficult to make. Identifying who is playing alone should not be too difficult, though children tend to switch quite frequently between being alone and being in a group. She will need to take measures of time spent alone and she may need to observe several playtimes in order to obtain a fair assessment. What will count as being bullied? As we said, she can't just stand by while bullying occurs. She may need to *code* behaviour (see pages 65–66) as aggressive (hitting, threatening, etc.) or she can ask individual children how much they feel they get bullied, remembering that children can use that term in widely differing circumstances.

4   Sheila will need to create a questionnaire which can be scored (see page 54) if she is to obtain quantitative differences between students

and truck drivers that can be meaningfully compared. Alternatively she might take a qualitative approach like Doug's below.

5 **Doug's approach is qualitative. This may or may not be a method recognised for coursework by your particular assessment body. Check first!**

If this is your approach then you need to be careful that your semi-structured interview technique is going to produce sufficient quantities of useful data, can be used on your chosen participants (e.g. is not too long-winded) and is different from a 'journalistic' form of interview. *Your* interview must be conducted with objective, non-value-laden questions that simply bring out the greatest possible amount of information from your interviewee. You do *not* want to solicit opinions in keeping with your own or those that you can be shocked at. Doug should be asking clear questions, with accompanying probes and prompts, that illuminate people's models of their environment. Doug should not respond with any emotion or leading questions that are prompted by his agreeing strongly or disagreeing with his interviewee.

How will the measures affect the hypothesis?

This question might seem odd. Surely the measures should be decided *in the light of* the hypothesis? This is true. If we want to show that the presence of an audience affects people's ability to count accurately then obviously we need to employ some simple measure of counting ability.

Very often though, in student projects, by the time the measures have been developed, it has become impossible to make the originally proposed hypothesis test. For example (and this is a true story using a fictitious name), Jill wanted to test the following hypothesis: 'People told that a woman was dressed revealingly will see her as more responsible for a sexual attack than those who were told she was dressed modestly'. Jill asked the question:

'Who was most responsible for the attack?' ☐ Man ☐ Woman

Of course, every participant ticked the 'Man' box. By using this crude categorical measure Jill had turned her test of the hypothesis above into a test of the following hypothesis: 'More people that were told a woman was dressed revealingly will see her as *most* responsible for a sexual attack than will those told she was dressed modestly'.

DIFFERENCE OR CORRELATION?

The most common shift in emphasis caused by a particular choice of variables is that from difference to correlation (see pages 46–47) or vice versa. For instance, very often people say they would like to correlate gender with smoking behaviour or being married with attitude to safe sex (for example). In these circumstances, because of the choice of categorical variables (gender; married or not) you just cannot correlate (see pages 93–96). These tests must be ones of difference – do males differ from females, marrieds from unmarrieds? In addition, suppose we just asked people whether they smoke or not. Again this is a categorical variable and we can't use it in a correlation. If we asked people this question and measured them on extroversion we could look at the difference between smokers and non-smokers on extroversion. We could not 'correlate' smoking with extroversion.

If we do want to correlate (look at the relationship between variable X and variable Y) then both variables X and Y must be at least at an ordinal level (see page 73), preferably interval level. So, if we want to 'correlate' gender in some way with, say, aggression, we would have to use one of the several 'masculinity–femininity' scales that exist, giving each person a score on masculinity–femininity, and we would need some quantitative measure of smoking, such as number of cigarettes smoked per day. Then we could correlate these two variables. Otherwise, with a categorical group variable (such as sex, vegetarian/meat-eater, student/non-student) we must use a hypothesis which is about group differences.

Starting out

It may seem as though we have put the cart before the horse here, by introducing some terms that have not appeared already. However, I hope you'll see that the considerations above simply must all be made before you even think about data gathering. You should return to this section when you have read through all the possibilities for design in the forthcoming chapters. If you have already studied research methods and are making practical plans for your research project, you should return to this discussion after you have made more concrete decisions. Bear these points in mind as you plan and you should not end up with an unworkable design or one that will produce meaningless data.

Experiments, quasi-experiments and non-experiments

What is a true experiment?

The main feature of an experiment is the attempt to identify cause and effect by holding every variable constant except one (the independent variable) and observing any consequent changes in the dependent variable. If such a relationship is demonstrated, we can argue that the independent variable has a direct effect on the dependent variable, though things are rarely as simple as that. To conduct a true experiment you must:

1   **manipulate an *independent variable***

2   **measure performance on a *dependent variable***

3   **neutralise possible *confounding variables.***

Point 3 is the hard part. A confounding variable is one which could invalidate your conclusion that the independent variable caused the dependent variable to change, since it might be the confounding variable that is responsible for the observed change. As an example, in Kelly's experiment (see page 12), the presence of the 'electrician' might have caused her to give briefer instructions to the participants in this condition. Alternatively, the presence of the 'electrician' might distract the participant from fully understanding the initial instructions. Participants might then take less time in the audience condition simply because they are doing the task the wrong way. Here, Kelly's conclusion that the presence of another *during the task* caused participants to take less time is wrong. It was the presence of another during the instruction period that caused the faster times. The results have been confounded by variation in the instruction phase.

RANDOM ALLOCATION OF PARTICIPANTS TO CONDITIONS

A very common cause of confounding is the differences between participants themselves. Suppose we had far better peg placers in the 'presence' condition than in the 'alone' condition. This would produce a faster performance in the 'presence' condition but not because of the 'electrician'.

To counteract the problem of these participant variables it is common to *randomly allocate* participants to conditions. This way any differences should be balanced out.

To randomly allocate Kelly's 20 participants to two conditions she could:

1 **generate a string of 20 random numbers and give each participant one of these in turn; start anywhere in Table A7 and move in one direction taking each number (alternatively, ask a computer programme (such as Excel) to generate the string or to randomly organise the original set of numbers).**

2 **organise the 20 participants according to the order of the random number they have received – put the top ten into one condition and the bottom ten into the other.**

A slightly less perfect way to randomly allocate, especially when you don't know how many participants will turn up, is to toss a coin for each participant but then to even up towards the end if too many have fallen into one of the conditions.

Controlling other confounding variables

Not all variables can be controlled. Having an audience naturally increases the amount of carbon dioxide in the room but we have to exercise discretion in our control. Such a minimal factor is hardly likely to affect performance on a peg-board task. However, we must also be cautious here. You should always look very carefully at possible confounding variables when you write the Discussion section of your report. Many apparently insignificant factors have been shown to affect performance and results. For instance, students told that their rats were 'bright' (when they weren't particularly) reported better maze running results than students not told this. The apparently 'minor' fact that students knew what was expected of their rats appeared subtly to affect the way in which they followed the experimenter's clear instructions to them on training the rats.

LABORATORY AND FIELD EXPERIMENTS

The definition of 'laboratory' as far as coursework projects are concerned is simply that a 'laboratory' study will take place in a room to which participants come and which has been arranged as far as possible to reduce the effects of any extraneous variables that might interfere with the action of the independent variable directly upon the dependent variable. It does not have to contain technical equipment and you do not need a white coat! The main advantage is the relatively strict control of variables. There are several possible disadvantages:

*   **your participants might feel uneasy in strange, formal surroundings and this might inhibit their performance**

*   **your participants might feel that their behaviour is being evaluated and this too might inhibit performance, especially if they are unfamiliar with psychology**

*   **conducting experiments in a laboratory can make the situation rather artificial (in the littering example (see Research in Practice 10) the scene is in many important ways different from a naturally occurring street situation)**

*   **participants might, for instance, feel that they must be on their best (or better) behaviour; they are in school/college after all.**

You will need to consider all these possibilities and decide whether, for your particular study, it is possible and more desirable to carry it out in the field, that is, in a natural environment for the participants. If you carry out a field study you will avoid some or all of the disadvantages of the laboratory listed above.

Studies in the field may be field experiments or they may be non-experiments such as an observation study. Your participants may or may not be aware that they are participating in an experiment. In the latter case you may well have to take note of additional ethical issues. An example of non-aware participants in a field experiment is the study proposed by Vijay in Research in Practice 13, page 23. The advantage is that these participants *must* be behaving naturally, unaffected by the knowledge of being in an experiment. The disadvantages of field studies and experiments generally concern the lack of control you will have over extraneous variables and over who participates in your study. In addition, you may well not be able to use elaborate or sensitive equipment and you will not be able to set the scene exactly as you might want it.

INDEPENDENT SAMPLES DESIGNS

If Kelly used different people in the 'presence' and 'alone' conditions, she would be running an *independent samples* design. It is also known as an 'unrelated design' because scores for individuals in one condition will be entirely unrelated to scores in the other condition. If you run this kind of experiment you would typically require an experimental group and a control group. The first group receives your 'treatment' (in the case above, presence of another) while the second group does not.

In a control condition participants experience everything that occurs in an experimental condition except for the 'treatment' variable.

The independent variable in an experiment is usually a categorical variable (see page 26) Here the two 'levels' (values) of the independent variable are 'presence' and 'alone'. Typically, we expect a difference in performance between the two groups on the dependent variable which might be time taken to complete the peg-board by using tweezers to place pins in all the holes; or it could be the number of pins placed in one minute.

Strengths of and problems with the independent samples design

The useful aspect of this design is that participants cannot possibly know what happened to the other group (unless they meet outside!). They cannot practise the task or worry about how well they'll do in the experimental condition, for instance. There are no *order effects* – effects from participating in two conditions in a particular order.

However, there is the problem of non-equivalent groups raised above. We said that Kelly could randomly allocate participants to conditions hoping that this will balance out any such person differences. This is not an ideal solution and a better alternative might be the 'repeated measures' design described below.

Alternatively she could try to demonstrate that she used equivalent groups by assessing participants on some important measure before starting the study. She could assess each participant on peg-placing before the experiment and show that there was initially no significant difference between them. She could go further and use these initial scores to allocate participants to conditions using a matched pairs procedure described later (see page 43).

In some designs you can only use an independent samples design, typically those employing a *vignette* approach. In the sexual attack research described on page 35, Jill used two vignettes. These were two short stories about her fictitious woman and her activities before being attacked. Both stories were identical except for the description of her dress – 'revealing' or 'modest'. These were the two levels of the independent variable. Clearly it would be pointless to ask people to rate the responsibility of the woman in one situation, then give participants the alternative description and ask them to rate again. A classic perception study design is to bias perception by showing an 'old' or 'young' version of the famous old/young lady drawing before showing the ambiguous version. Another is to show numbers or letters before showing an ambiguous **13**. In such cases you are forced to use different participants in each condition.

REPEATED MEASURES DESIGN

A version of the audience experiment that would avoid the problem of participant variation would be to have each participant perform in both conditions. This way we are measuring each participant's performance in one condition against that same participant's performance in the second condition. This *repeated measures* design gives us a much more powerful design than that of independent samples. For the statistical analysis we can simply say 'To what extent did each person improve?' rather than, 'Did one group do better than the other?' In this design we look at the difference between each participant's performances. Because we look at results in *pairs* – the difference between conditions for each participant – this design belongs to a category known as *related*.

Strengths of and problems with the repeated measures design

We have just looked at the main strength of this design. Differences between conditions cannot be the result of differences between participant groups. A further advantage is that the design is economical on participants – for each participant we can persuade to join our experiment we get two scores, one for each condition.

We have already mentioned one of the main problems with this design – that of order effects. Participants may improve through practice or through gaining knowledge of your experimental purpose. They may deteriorate in performance if your conditions are rather long-winded and they have to go through them twice. If all participants were to perform in the control (no audience) condition first we might get the confounding problem of practice outlined in Figure 6.1.

If you are running a repeated measures experiment such as this one you should consider ways to avoid these possible order effects. There are several practical solutions, including the following.

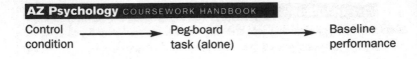

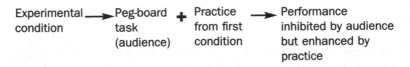

Figure 6.1 Addition of practice in the second condition of a repeated measures experiment

- **Counterbalance by having half your participants (randomly selected) perform in the 'audience' (experimental) condition *before* the 'alone' (control) condition. This way practice effects will not disappear but they should be balanced out across conditions so that any real effect from the audience should still be left as an overall difference between performance in the two conditions.**

- **Establish a baseline. Remove practice effects by having participants perform the task many times in pre-experimental trials until there is no more improvement in their performance through practice. This way any effect of the audience should be written on top of two samples of near perfect performance.**

- **Where each condition consists of several trials you can simply mix all these trials together in a random manner, known as *randomisation*. For instance, suppose you are investigating differences in time taken to solve anagrams of emotional and non-emotional words. You have several anagrams to be solved in each category. Here you can simply mix all the anagrams together in a random order so that the participant cannot guess which type of word the next anagram will produce. This neatly avoids practice effects but also any expectancy effect where the participant knows what is expected on the next trial. However, you have to measure time taken to solve each separate anagram.**

MATCHED PAIRS DESIGN

On some occasions it is possible to get the best of both worlds in terms of repeated measures *and* independent samples designs. An example is given in Research in Practice 15. Since, again, we look at differences between pairs of scores, this design is another kind of related design. It has the advantage that order effects are avoided whilst keeping effects of participant variation to a minimum.

Research in Practice 15

Tammy wanted to show that people would solve anagrams faster where the target words are grouped into categories. For instance, experimental participants would be given five anagrams of animals, then four of vegetables, and so on. Control group participants would receive the same anagrams but in a randomised sequence. Tammy also reasoned that English ability would be an individual difference that might interfere with her results. She asked those that were willing to provide their mock English GCSE result. She paired the top two of her participants, dividing them at random so that one went to the experimental condition and the other went to the control condition. She then did the same thing with the next two highest and so on. When she analysed the results she looked at the difference in number of anagrams solved between the two participants in the first pair, the two in the second pair and so on, using a *related* test of significance.

SINGLE CASE AND SMALL *N* DESIGNS

Although most experiments use a number of participants in order to observe an overall effect, treating the samples as being representative of an underlying population, many experiments in the applied field are used on single participants or on a few cases ('small *N*'). The focus here is on each individual and whether a specific independent variable has an effect. For example, a clinical psychologist working with a disruptive child might be interested in whether a 'treatment' – small rewards for staying on task or in the classroom seat – is having a marked effect on the target behaviour. Typically the researcher would establish a baseline for the target behaviour to be reduced (or increased), then apply the treatment, then check by removing

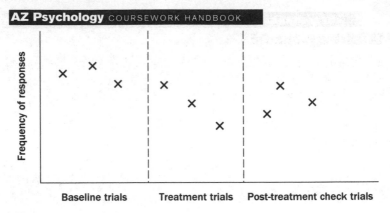

Figure 6.2

the treatment to see whether behaviour returns to its original level. Such a design is known as an A-B-A design, with the two A phases being without treatment and the B phase being where the treatment is applied. An analysis of results would typically take the form of a time series chart as in the figure above where there are three trials in each phase.

Of course you will not be able to employ a 'treatment' in this applied and professional manner. However, you could use this approach with one or a few participants. You could investigate, for instance, the effect of calming music on the performance of a difficult manual task such as the wiggly wire task seen at village fêtes or simply threading beads onto a string. Alternatively you might investigate the effects of giving a visual aid to a participant who has to learn lists of ten words in a new (to them) foreign language. In each case you must put enough trials into the first phase to establish the participant's baseline of performance – their level of performance, once practised, which is at a steady level and prior to any 'treatment'.

The results from such experiments can be discussed in some depth. You can check for instance whether there is a 'tail off' in the third phase or whether, apparently, the effect from the 'treatment' phase persists. However, the results are not always appropriate for a test of significant difference. Significance tests are usually performed on data from *groups* of participants or on the results of a substantial number of trials with a single participant. Hence you should check that your syllabus permits you to submit a quantitative-type assignment with no inferential statistics.

Quasi-experiments

If you carry out a true experiment you will manipulate an independent variable, and you will hold all other variables constant or balanced as far as is reasonably possible. Remember, the reason for this strict procedure is that we are trying to isolate cause and effect. We are trying to demonstrate without ambiguity that our independent variable has a direct effect on our dependent variable. Any lack of control of variables in a research study is a possible source of confounding. There may be alternative explanations for our effect. Such possible sources of confounding are known as 'threats to the validity' of the findings from the study.

Very often it is not possible to achieve the desired level of experimental control yet we can still be fairly certain that an independent variable affected a dependent variable. Such studies are often called *quasi-experiments*. The skilled researcher can often introduce some extra form of assessment in order to compensate for the lack of control. Often, however, this is physically impossible or, for the student doing early research in psychology, there is not the time nor the professional experience or elaborate resources to make this compensation.

Quasi-experiments tend to occur more frequently in the field (outside the laboratory, in the natural environment of the participants) where control is difficult. They also occur where to control would be unethical. For instance, we could not inflict a great deal of stress upon participants in a laboratory (or classroom), in order to investigate the effect on reasoning ability. However, we could ask people in high and low stress occupations to complete a test for us.

THE PROBLEM OF NON-EQUIVALENT GROUPS

A very common lack of control is that of not being able to allocate participants to conditions of the experiment at random. For instance, in Laura's study (Research in Practice 1, page 7) using litter on the floor and observing whether participants dropped their crisp packet, she was unable to allocate participants to conditions at random. She had asked for volunteers to come on two different lunch hours, one when the room was kept tidy and the other when it was littered. She did not know, in advance, who would be able to attend. The problem was that it could be that those who turned up for the first lunch time with the tidy room might have been generally tidier or more litter conscious people. This could confound the results of the experiment.

A B C D E F G H I J K L M N O P Q R S T U V W X Y Z

45

How could Laura compensate here? Well, she could ask each participant to make a self-assessment on general tidiness or to answer a questionnaire on tidiness and care of the environment. She could then show that the two groups did not differ on this variable yet still performed differently under the experimental conditions. However, for basic psychology coursework this might be up at the high end of complexity. It is important, though, at least to recognise the possible sources of confounding in your design. This is done in the Discussion section of your report.

NATURAL EXPERIMENTS

Another 'lack of control' putting studies into the quasi-experiment category are those research situations in which the researcher does not control the independent variable. Suppose you knew in advance that your local council was about to introduce rumble strips on the approach to a traffic junction. You could measure the speed of cars before and after the strips are introduced and provide evidence for the hypothesis that an intrusive noise has an effect on driver behaviour. Of course you would have to compensate for possible differences between the observed samples by ensuring that you use the same time of day, weather conditions, lighting conditions and so on. Another example might be where some pupils in a local school (possibly yours) have attended a cycle safety course. You could observe whether these riders, compared with a control group, carry out more safety precautions (such as carrying proper lights, wearing reflective clothing, looking carefully, etc.). You could compensate for the fact that the 'treatment group' might have been more conscientious in the first place by comparing behaviour before and after the training course takes place.

Notice that, with these natural experiments, there is an identifiable independent variable or 'treatment' for one group but it is not one that you control. Notice also that these examples do not include the situation where you simply compare differences between two identifiably different groups of people. In this case the people have usually not participated in any kind of experiment at all. We shall go on to consider such studies next.

Non-experimental studies ('correlational' and group difference research)

Many studies cannot be said to involve the use of an independent variable at all. Judy's study (Research in Practice 14) looked at differences between two existing groups of people – extroverts and introverts. This personality difference does not constitute an 'independent variable' in the experimental sense. There is not a 'treatment' here that one group has undergone, one which is different for the other group. This is a personality difference identified *post hoc* and such studies are sometimes called *ex post facto* (after the fact) studies.

These non-experimental studies are also sometimes called 'correlational', meaning that we are just looking at existing relationships between variables. The term is misleading however as the statistical procedure of correlation (see pages 93–96) is not always involved. In the case of extroversion/introversion and the BA tail-fins Judy can do one of two things.

1 **Split the sample into two groups, extroverts and introverts, and conduct a test of group difference in tail-fin liking scores (e.g. Mann–Whitney – see page 85)**

2 *Correlate scores on extroversion/introversion with scores on tail-fin liking.*

If there is a relationship between extroversion and tail-fin liking then both these studies should come up with pretty well the same level of significance, as long as they use the data from all the participants. Both studies investigate whether there is an association between extroversion and tail-fin liking.

WHAT DOES A CORRELATION SHOW?

If you conduct a study which uses a statistical correlation you will have two measures for each participant in your study (i.e. not just categories). The measures will be of two variables thought to be related, for instance numerical and verbal reasoning ability. Your correlation result will answer the question:

do participants tend to score as high on one test as on the other?

To the extent that this is true, the closer your calculated *positive correlation* will be to one. If high scores on one variable tend to be associated with low scores on the other, the relationship is known as a *negative correlation*.

Research in Practice 16
A study using correlation

Matt wanted to investigate the theory of cognitive dissonance. He reasoned that the more cigarettes that ▶

Continued

people smoke the less inclined they would be to accept the serious health risks associated with smoking. He used an attitude scale (see pages 53–5) which gave a total scale on 'health risk belief' and he asked people how many cigarettes per day they smoked (non-smokers were not included since they would form a large group all on the same 'score' of zero). He then had two scores for each participant: score on health belief and score on smoking. On the health belief scale, a high score implied that the person very much believed smoking was injurious to health. Hence, Matt predicted that high scores on smoking would tend to be paired with low scores on health belief and vice versa. This then was a prediction of a *negative correlation*.

There are very many studies which you can carry out in this general area of research design. The examples concerning divergent thinking (pages 8–9) belong here. We can look at the correlation between convergent and divergent thinking scores or between the divergent thinking scores of parents and their children.

INTERPRETATION PROBLEMS WITH NON-EXPERIMENTAL STUDIES

Suppose we were interested in the theory that convergent and divergent thinking are entirely different and unrelated abilities. If we conduct a correlation study what would we expect to find? We would expect a correlation, among the population as a whole, of zero. We said earlier (see page 22) that you should not try to produce such null results. You could instead, here, predict that Maths students will score higher on divergent thinking than Arts students and vice versa for divergent thinking.

Should such a difference occur you could argue that you have conducted a quasi-experiment in which students have been 'treated' with either Maths training or Arts training, and that the training has caused them to become either better at divergent thinking or better at convergent thinking. The trouble is that we could also argue that people who were naturally good at divergent thinking would be more attracted to Arts subjects.

So-called 'correlational' studies, in fact any study which is not a true experiment, have the weakness that you have not controlled an independent variable in order to observe the consequent effect upon the dependent variable. We often cannot tell the direction of cause. Did variable A influence variable B, did variable B influence variable A, or did both variables get influenced by some other variable (perhaps choosing Arts subjects and being a divergent thinker are results of parental/school influence)? It would be unethical, of course, as well as impractical, to take people and randomly allocate them to a Maths or an Arts course and see what effects on thinking this has. However, you *could*, if you have the time, give volunteers a short course in divergent thinking tasks to see whether they improve on a divergent thinking test or surpass the performance of non-trained participants.

Where we cannot conduct this kind of controlled experimental study we usually have the problem of ambiguity in our interpretation, that is, what influenced what? However this ambiguity is only a matter of degree. There are always certain 'threats to validity', even in a well-controlled experiment. Then again, what is usually not ambiguous is that the dependent variable changes after the independent variable has been manipulated. In a quasi-experiment we can take pre-measures of the dependent variable to show that it does change after the treatment. For instance, we could, if we had the time, measure Arts and Maths students' divergent thinking before they start their courses. However, if we only conduct a correlation or group difference study, measuring the divergent thinking ability of existing Arts and Maths students, then we are measuring *ex post facto* (after the fact) and must always recognise that B could cause A as much as A might have caused B – that is, divergent thinking ability might have influenced the choice of an Arts course rather than the Arts course influencing the divergent thinking ability (or a bit of both?).

Is mine an experiment?

You do not need to get involved in debates about whether or not your proposed study is or is not a true experiment. If your syllabus demands an experiment then the best thing to do is to make absolutely sure that what you do clearly is an experiment. If no particular design is prescribed, save that it be quantitative, then any of the examples given would do. However, what is essential is that you do attempt to identify, accurately, the type of design you have used and that you get to grips with all the 'threats' associated with this type of design that might undermine the validity of your findings. Always keep asking yourself, especially as you come to write up the critique of your project (see page 113):

> what else could have caused this effect, or, what might have prevented the expected effect from showing up?

Surveys and questionnaires

What is a survey study?

Surveys usually gather data on a large number of respondents, anything from a few hundred to many thousands. In your research work you are unlikely to question this many respondents, unless you pool data from several class colleagues where each student questions, say, 30 respondents. However, most examination boards would accept as a 'survey' or 'questionnaire' type study those where you investigate a difference by using your questionnaire or interview procedure on, say, 15 members of two groups. These could be Maths teachers and English teachers, for instance, or mothers and fathers. Rather than look for a difference, however, formal surveys can be used in entirely descriptive studies, where the researchers report on percentages of people having this or that opinion or possessing this or that type of property.

The use of questionnaires in surveys and experiments

A questionnaire is a set of questions put to a 'respondent' (the usual name for a participant in a survey- or questionnaire-using study). Questionnaires are often used in surveys. However, you might also use a questionnaire as part of an experiment. Here it will be a measure of the dependent variable. For instance, you might ask people to complete a questionnaire measuring attitude to refugees before and after they view a television programme which describes dreadful conditions which refugees have fled. The questionnaire can serve one of two purposes: as a measuring instrument, or as an information-gathering device. It can be used in many types of research study, including the experiment, but is more often used as the data-gathering tool in a survey or series of interviews and we shall concentrate mainly on this use here.

The questionnaire as a measuring instrument

Have a look at the study described in Research in Practice 17, page 52. Here we have an example of a questionnaire being used to measure the dependent variable in a 'vignette' type experiment. In such experiments (very easily run by psychology students) the independent variable is the alteration of just one item of information. In this case the students have used the questionnaire for several purposes. One is to make sure that they are aware of the gender of the author. Second, there are a couple of 'decoy' questions to take the emphasis away from gender so that participants will not realise (at the time) what the experiment is actually about. Third, they have taken measures on several dependent variables: liking for the article, quality of the article, author's expertise and effectiveness. To analyse their results they may need to run an appropriate significance test on each of these dependent variables in turn.

ASSESSMENT ITEMS

If you use a scale to measure a dependent variable such as 'author's expertise' (see Research in Practice 17), there are several things to take into account. You can label every point of a small scale as these students did. However, it is often more effective to give people plenty of space and to label only either end of a 'bi-polar' type scale. For example:

Please mark on the scale below your feelings about classical music:

1	2	3	4	5	6	7	8	9	10
really don't like									like very much

Using 1 to 100 is a bit pointless since the extra points do not deliver any greater accuracy. The scale is not interval (see page 26) and should best be treated as ordinal in the analysis. You cannot claim that one person's six is 'twice' another's three and it is even doubtful that all sixes are 'above' all fives. What certainly makes sense is to use the same scale for each dependent variable so that your participants do not have to keep adjusting to new instructions.

Research in Practice 17

Rikki and Tanya tested the hypothesis that when people assess the quality of an article, their judgement can be affected by knowledge of the author's gender. They used a newspaper article on a gender neutral subject (public ▶

Continued

transport). Half their participants were told the article was written by John Williams while the other half were told the author was Jenny Williams. After reading the article the participants were given the following questionnaire:

a What is the title of the article?

....

b What was the author's name?

....

c How old was he/she?

....

d Where did he/she live?

....

On a scale where 1 = very low, 2 = low, 3 = medium, 4 = high and 5 = very high, give a rating of:

		Rating
1	Your liking for the article	☐
2	The quality of the article	☐
3	The author's expertise in the subject	☐
4	The author's effectiveness in convincing the reader	☐

ATTITUDE SCALES AND SELF-DESCRIPTIONS

Attitude scales

An attitude scale measures people's attitude towards a particular issue. It can take several forms but a very commonly used approach is to give respondents a set of statements (each a single 'item' in the scale) to which they respond with one of a given set of answers along a directional scale. For instance, a scale measuring attitude to refugees might ask people to choose a response from:

strongly agree	agree	undecided	disagree	strongly disagree
1	2	3	4	5

to items such as:

a   Refugees are usually escaping from very dangerous conditions (positive)

b   Refugees are very often just looking for jobs in this country (negative).

Such a scale would normally consist of 20 or more similar items. All the items must be assessed on the same scale because then it is possible to add up all the scores on each item to produce an overall attitude score for each respondent. To develop such a scale you must pay attention to the following.

1   All items must be statements not questions.

2   Respondents must answer all items. You cannot compare the score of someone who has answered only 18 items with those of people who have answered 20. Eighteen items allows a maximum score of only 90 whereas the full score possible here is 100. Hence it is important to check that every item has been answered and to avoid including items that some respondents may refuse, or be unable, to answer.

3   Use as many negative as positive items. The first item above is positive towards refugees whereas the second is negative. If you use items that are all in one direction (either negative or positive) then you run the risk of response bias.

4   Use stronger and weaker statements, equally balanced among positive and negative items as far as possible. For instance 'refugees should be sent back immediately no matter what their circumstances' is a strong negative whereas 'refugees are sometimes not genuine' is a weak negative statement.

5   When you score each respondent's answers you must first reverse the scoring on either all the positive items or all the negative items. If we want a high score to indicate a positive attitude towards refugees then we want a high score on item (a) above. However, with the scoring scale as used above, the respondent strongly agreeing with the item scores only 1 (rather than 5). For positive items then we would reverse the scoring so that 1 = 5, 2 = 4, 3 = 3, 4 = 2 and 5 = 1. On item (b)

the person positive towards refugees will initially score 5 for strongly disagree, and therefore responses to negative items should be left as they are and not reversed.

6   You could use a different response scale, though the one above is common and usually adequate. However, care must be taken with interpretation of the 'undecided' point. For all we know, the person, when decided, may take a strong position on the item. The label for the mid-point could be 'neutral' but this is ambiguous. The respondent may have no view at all or may be able to see both sides and therefore is 'undecided'. You could omit the neutral point entirely but this forces people off the fence and may result in a nil response. As we saw above, all items must be answered or else that respondent's results must be discarded. Some people use a 1 to 7 or 1 to 6 (no mid-point) scale.

7   Statements must be unambiguous, clear and simple – see below.

Self-descriptions

The response scale above (known as a Likert-type scale) can also be used when asking people to rate themselves on certain personality characteristics. Suppose you hypothesised that second-born children are more confident than first-born children. You could assess confidence using statements such as:

● **I never hesitate when making a telephone call to a stranger**

● **I always look away from people in a lift.**

These statements can be responded to using a re-worded **Likert scale**:

Very like me	Like me	A bit like me	Not very much like me	Not like me at all
1	2	3	4	5

The items can be both negative and positive, as before, and, after reversing one of these sets of items, the score for each item can be added to produce an overall score on 'confidence'.

Creating useful questionnaire or scale items

Whether you are creating an assessment scale (using items to be agreed or disagreed with) or using actual questions, you will need to take note of several principles in order to make your items clear and unambiguous. We want items that most people will interpret, though not answer, in the same way. We'll assume below, mostly, that you are creating a Likert-type scale though most of the points also apply to survey and interview questions. For instance 'Refugees are usually escaping terrible conditions' can be re-phrased as a real question 'Do you think refugees are escaping terrible conditions?'

In devising your questions you should pay attention to the following possible pitfalls which also apply to any *interview* technique.

1   Complexity

Keep items as simple as possible so that respondents can understand the statement and interpret it in the same way as do other respondents.

2   Double-barrelled items

Related to simplicity is the need not to ask two questions in one. For instance:

refugees are escaping danger and we have a duty to protect them

is an item where some respondents might want to agree that refugees are escaping danger yet not agree that we have a duty to protect them.

3   Technical terms

Another factor contributing to difficulty and complexity is the use of technical terms. For instance in the item:

anti-refugee attitudes are caused by ethnocentric bias

you may well understand the term 'ethnocentric' but your respondent may not have a clue.

4   Ambiguity

Try hard to think how people with either extreme of attitude would think about each item. For instance, you might produce, as a pro-refugee item:

the children of refugees need education.

However, a person who is anti refugee might still agree with this item, having in mind the extra cost that the taxpayer might have to bear.

5   Negative grammar

Because we need both positive and negative items it is often tempting to change positive to negative by using negative terms, such as 'not'.

However this can produce quite awkward items that are easily misunderstood. For instance, the following 'pro' item, produced from an original 'anti' item, forces respondents to juggle with two negative terms:

>   refugees should not be discouraged from claiming benefits.

Better would be:

>   refugees should be encouraged to claim benefits.

6   Leading questions

These should always be avoided. A leading question is one where you direct the respondent towards what appears to be the desired response. For instance, if you were using direct questions and not statements, the following item:

>   don't you think refugees should be sent straight back home?

forces the person who is generally pro-refugee onto the back foot. They have to come back and defend their positions, as it were.

7   Obscurity

Don't ask questions that respondents are unlikely to be able to answer, such as: 'How many times have you visited the doctor in the last five years?'

8   Invasion of privacy

A question like 'Have you ever suffered from a mental illness or condition?' may not be asked by students conducting a project. It is an invasion of the respondent's privacy. You should always get your tutor to check out your questions where you are unsure about their ethical nature (or do this anyway, just in case).

9   General English

Be sure to use objective English language and not slang or colloquial terms. Here are some features to avoid:

i   Racism is down to poor education.

ii   Do you believe in physical punishment?

iii The amount of refugees arriving in Britain is low.

iv   Racist people could of had a poor education.

In (i) the phrase 'down to' is colloquial and needs replacing by, for instance, 'caused by'. In (ii) the answer could be 'yes' even if the person doesn't favour the administration of physical punishment. 'Do you believe in ...' is colloquial and could be more accurately phrased as 'Do you agree with?' In (iii) 'amount' should be 'number' and in (iv) 'could of' should be 'could have'.

Is this being picky and destroying the natural interest and creativity of the questionnaire-producing psychology student? Well, perhaps, but the argument for good English, apart from allowing you to express yourself accurately (good practice for exams), is that otherwise people just might not take your questionnaire seriously. If you want respondents to answer genuinely and to take your project as a serious piece of psychological research then you don't want to have them chuckling at poor English and dismissing your work as 'amateurish'. Hence, in order to produce a good questionnaire in this respect (and this advice goes for all written work in fact):

* **use a spell checker but remember that it will pass correctly spelled but unintended words (e.g. 'to' instead of 'too')**
* **read all your sentences slowly out loud to yourself – if you don't understand them or find them awkward or 'odd', so will your respondents**
* **get a friend to read them, or a parent, or someone you know who has good English**
* **get your tutor to check the questionnaire before gathering data with it.**

The questionnaire as an information-gathering device

You may be using a questionnaire or interview as a straightforward information-gathering technique, rather than as a measuring instrument for one specific attribute. In this case there is a primary golden rule:

ask only for what you need.

Students often say, when asked why a certain item is in their questionnaire, 'Oh I just thought I might need it'. For instance, in a questionnaire asking about physical punishment one student asked for people's ethnicity, the number of A levels they had and the type of work they did. However, none of these items of information was required in order to test her hypothesis that mothers and fathers differed in the amount of physical punishment they might administer to sons and daughters. You should always plan your hypotheses and therefore your data analysis before constructing and using your questionnaire.

MINESTRONE QUESTIONNAIRES AND 'FISHING'

Some questionnaires are like minestrone soup: they contain a higedly-pigledy mix of qualitatively different types of item, mostly thrown in because 'it seemed like a good idea' at the time of construction. Having asked about gender, economic and marital status, salary, number of siblings, etc. etc. there is often the temptation to conduct a significance test on all these group differences 'just to see if there's a difference'. This is known as 'fishing' and has serious implications in significance testing. The very nature of significance testing (see page 79) means that for every 20 tests you conduct on pairs of samples taken from the same population you will, on average, find one 'significant' result. This is not, of course, a result which shows evidence of a difference between populations. We have already said the data were gathered randomly from the *same* population (think of a coffee purchaser taking random samples from a sack of coffee beans). If you didn't know this however you would assume, according to the rules of significance testing, that there was indeed an underlying significant difference. In fact you would have committed what is known as a *Type I error*. The more tests you conduct, even on randomly selected data, the more risk you run of obtaining a Type I error – a 'fluke', random, but large enough difference to 'count' as significant. Hence, if your questionnaire contains many different items on which you choose to conduct significance tests you are more likely (than with a few questions) to obtain a 'fluke' result. You should recognise this in your Discussion of Results if you are in this position but it would be better to focus your questionnaire *only* on areas where specific predictions can be made from the theory and research in your Introduction.

QUESTION FORMATS

When using a questionnaire or interview as an information-gathering device there are several possible formats for your questions. Suppose you simply want to know what methods students use to help them revise for exams. You can include open-ended items (e.g. 'Tell me what you do when ...'). These generate qualitative data and are rather harder to analyse than closed items. The latter come in several forms – here are a few examples:

Projects in Practice

a When you revise do you listen to music?   yes/no

b Tick which of the following learning aids you use when revising:

short notes ☐   full notes ☐   spider-grams ☐

lists ☐   essay plans ☐   highlighting text ☐

Other (give detail) ....

c Give a rank from 1 to 5 to each of the following items in order of preference where 1 is your preferred approach:

Rank

Reading my list of notes silently ☐

Reading my list of notes out loud ☐

Paraphrasing my list of notes ☐

Copying out my list of notes ☐

Listening to my notes from a tape ☐

d On average, how many hours a day do you revise? ☐

Note that some of these items make it hard to give each person a 'score' and then to conduct a significance test. However, you may only want to produce a descriptive account in which case you will be able to present your data in terms of percentages, mean ranks, frequencies and so on.

What is your sample?

This issue also applies to any of the studies so far mentioned in this chapter. You must always ask yourself, before conducting a research study 'In what sorts of people am I interested?' You can't conduct a study which gathers data on 'people in general' because your sample will be only a tiny proportion of the world's population! Think whether you want mainly students, mainly older people, members of both genders and so on. Also think carefully whether you will be able, realistically, to find enough of the sort of person you are aiming to question. For instance, will you be able to find many left-handers, 6-year-old children, doctors?

Very often there will be no specific sampling method because you have used an *'opportunity sample'* – those people you could get hold of. This fact is important. Friends and acquaintances are not just anybody. **Never** claim that your sample was 'randomly selected' unless it really was. Asking people on the street is not random but 'haphazard' selection. Random selection is a scientific procedure which involves ensuring that every *individual in the target population has an equal chance of being selected*. To randomly select 50 students from the A level students at your college, for instance, you would need to give *all* A level students a number, then make sure that 50 of these were selected at random using a computer program, random number tables, or by drawing 50 numbers from all the numbers shuffled in a box.

Specific methods, intended to draw representative samples, include quota, stratified and cluster sampling. A stratified sample of Psychology A level students by gender would include 80 per cent females and 20 per cent males if the entire A level Psychology population were 80 per cent female and 20 per cent male, with random selection within the male and female populations. It is worth consulting a research methods text (e.g. Coolican, 1999) for more detail on accurate sampling, including non-representative methods such as 'snowball sampling'.

Obtaining your sample

You can use several means to find respondents and each has advantages and disadvantages. Here are some suggestions and hints.

Table 2 Means of obtaining your sample

Face to face (e.g. in college canteen)	Time consuming; high response rate; less misunderstanding or non-completion of items; be exceedingly polite if asking strangers and carry identity; announce your aim and institution, if outside it.
Post	Expensive; lower response rate; possible misunderstanding of items; include SAE and remind after a week or so.
E-mail	Similar to post but quicker; excludes those without access.
Whole class or lecture group	Efficient. Seek permission from the tutor first! If a school class, make sure parents and head are aware.
Telephone	Expensive; ethically questionable if 'cold calling'.
Leave questionnaire to be picked up	Very low response rate; possible misunderstanding of items; make it very visible and attractive.

Identify your questionnaire!

Whatever the purpose of your questionnaire, if it is to be distributed to people for completion make sure that you put at the top of it:

- **who you are**
- **the title and purpose of the questionnaire**
- **your school/college**
- **a return address.**

Observation studies

In a sense, any study you carry out will involve some form of observation. You will have to observe participants' reactions and make recordings. However, an 'observation study', in the sense of conducting coursework, will usually involve you in the recording and analysis of relatively unconstrained segments of human behaviour. Whereas in an experiment you would, for instance, count up the number of correct memory responses after your participant has left, in an observation study you might make records (on paper or electronically) of your participants' behaviour as they attempt to tell a colleague about what they did last weekend. In the observation study you might be interested in the number of times they hesitate, the movements of their hands when they discuss embarrassing incidents, when they make eye contact and when they appear to find this difficult. You can observe very simple aspects of behaviour. For instance, you could simply record whether or not a person drops on the ground a leaflet that you have just given to them.

However, an 'observation study' usually entails the recording of more complex, free-flowing behaviour often using a specially designed *coding system* to select several aspects of this behaviour for special analysis. Included here, for example, would be observations of:

- **two people holding a conversation – recording various aspects of their non-verbal behaviour such as eye contact, gestures, distance the two keep apart**

- **children during messy play – recording disgust, pleasure or humour reactions, attempts to keep clean, imaginative suggestions made by each child, interactions between genders**

- **people in a meeting – recording types of comment made (e.g. supportive, critical), methods to gain 'the stage', gender differences (e.g. ways men might undermine women; use of 'flirtatious' gestures).**

Laboratory observations

Observing participants in the 'laboratory' (e.g. the classroom where you have set up a situation in which to observe participants' behaviour) has certain advantages. You need not transport awkward equipment. You can record, with permission, their behaviour using a hidden camera so that the behaviour may be analysed with plenty of time later on and so that the participant does not feel intimidated by the presence of the equipment. You can control most other variables that might otherwise interfere; those that might distract your participant, such as suddenly opening doors or people interrupting.

Naturalistic observation

The trouble with observation in the laboratory is that the behaviour you observe almost certainly will not be what you might observe when people are behaving normally in their natural environment (also see the points made on page 39). Observing, unobtrusively, what people normally do, in their everyday environment, is known as *naturalistic observation*. There are some drawbacks, however.

First, you must make sure that your observation is ethical. Making notes on what people do in an obviously exposed public place, without intervention, is generally considered fair play. The people would anyway have behaved like that and anyone at all could be making notes. However, if you intervene in the situation then ethical issues become central. Asking people to change a pound for two 50 pence pieces might be considered trivial. Staging a mock accident or arranging for a person to act as though they were sick in order to see whether people come to help, is a serious intervention in people's everyday lives.

Second, you cannot control what happens in a naturalistic setting. If you intend to observe how children interact in twos, threes and fours, what happens if there are no children playing in pairs? If you are observing how long a child stays 'on task', you can do nothing about the fact that a friend might intervene, thus artificially shortening the on-task time. In other words, in a natural setting there can be many uncontrolled extraneous variables that might confound your findings. Your task is to try to anticipate and account for as many of these as possible.

The advantages of naturalistic observation are many. You are observing what normally happens, not behaviour which has been unnaturally requested in an unfamiliar setting. Some behaviour can only be observed in a natural setting.

Most activities concerning children fall into this category. Though you can ask children questions in any environment, you can only observe playground interaction in the playground.

Structuring your observations

Before you start any kind of observation, but especially if you are using a naturalistic approach, you must carefully define what it is that you will record. Your observations must be structured. It is no use simply making notes on 'My cousin's baby at play'. You need a research question and you need to gather data in an organised manner so that they can be *coded* in order to support your research predictions.

Suppose, in order to support a variety of hypotheses, a group of students wanted to observe the following sorts of behaviour:

* **aggression in the playground**
* **caring behaviour in the nursery**
* **recognition of a smile**
* **difficulty parking a car rear end first.**

In order to record behaviour in these categories it will be necessary first to produce some operational definitions – see page 22. What will count as 'aggression'? A possible check sheet for recording instances of aggression in the playground is shown on the next page.

What would count as 'caring' behaviour? This is an even broader and possibly more vague category of behaviour. Perhaps we could start to categorise 'caring' actions to include: caressing, tending another when hurt or upset, sharing, giving, expressing sympathy and so on. Even these categories however will need some further refinement. When does a hand hold become too tight to count as 'caring', for instance?

Recognition of a smile is a simpler category but what will count? A smile back, a 'friendly' nod, a word of greeting and so on?

'Difficulty' parking a car really can be a subjective judgement. Obvious instances will be those where the person takes a long time and is clearly frustrated. However, should we also include instances of bad parking (car skewed across lines) even if the driver appears happy with the position? Do we have a criterion number of back and forths before coding a manoeuvre as 'difficult'?

USING AN OBSERVATION CHECK SHEET

Behaviour can be coded 'live' by using an observation check sheet like that shown below. A single child's behaviour can be observed for certain periods of time (all equal) either picked at random over one or several sessions, or associated with different activities – see 'sampling behaviour' below. Your observation sheet should be *piloted* by trying it out beforehand to see whether all likely categories have been included and to see how difficult it is to complete as children interact with one another.

An observation check sheet for recording behaviour

Observation on: _____ Date: _____ Room: _____ Activity: _____												
Time:												
Hard hit												
Soft hit												
Pinch												
Kick												
Wrestle												
Hold												
Take/snatch												
Shout												
Reject												
Face/gesture												
Other*												
Notes (*):												

VIDEO RECORDINGS

Of course life would be a lot easier if you made a video recording of the children's behaviour then completed your coding at a later date, giving yourself plenty of time to check over all the detail, replay the tape and so on. However, there are some pitfalls associated with this method (especially with children):

- **the presence of the camera can be quite distracting and children might 'play up' to it**

- it is easy to record a lot of behaviour then find it hard and very time consuming to code all the data

- mechanical errors are easy to make – e.g. no tape running in the machine

- the need to hide the camera might result in an obscured view or a camera left running in a nursery room might end up being obscured as children or staff move objects around

- ethical issues if the camera is hidden; obtaining permission from parents or participants.

Research in Practice 18

A naturalistic observation study on giving and leadership

Orla decided to observe 3½ to 4½-year-old children in a nursery where she worked on a voluntary basis after college. Since she was a known helper, parents were quite willing to sign a sheet permitting her to make observations of their children under supervision.

Orla had read of a theory claiming that children who engage in a high degree of 'giving behaviour', at nursery age, are more likely to show good leadership skills as they develop. She decided to test this hypothesis by correlating scores from her own observations on giving with ratings given by the nursery supervisor on the extent to which each child exhibited leadership behaviour.

In order to operationalise her measures Orla allocated one mark for 'giving' each time a child gave or attempted to give voluntarily an object to another child, so long as this was not part of a game or task that the children were engaged in. The theory had claimed that children do this quite often in free play and that it is the quite un-prompted act of giving that evolves into leadership qualities. For her 'leadership' score she asked the supervisor to rate each child on a scale of 1 to 20 according to how often and how well they tended to initiate play, take the lead or give instructions. Included in her description was the requirement that 'leadership' be

Continued

effective; simply shouting instructions or requests, without compliance from other children, did not count.

On the days of the observation Orla was introduced to the children and they were told that Orla would be 'taking some notes on how children play', and they were politely asked not to disturb her during this time. Orla promised to play with the children when she had finished. The observations were conducted by selecting six girls and six boys at random from the whole group. Each of these was observed for two 10-minute sessions of free play. The child to be observed for each 10-minute session was selected from a randomly ordered list until all had been observed twice.

From the raw data Orla averaged the number of 'giving' actions and conducted a Spearman correlation (see page 94) on the pairs of giving and leadership scores.

DECIDING HOW TO TAKE OBSERVATIONS – SAMPLING BEHAVIOUR

In Research in Practice 18 we saw that Orla found a way to observe different children at different times in a fair and unbiased manner. The problem is that in a naturalistic setting you will probably not be able to observe all the people all the time. If your hypothesis entails the observation of a number of adults or children then you need a method to sample behaviour in order to get a picture of what the typical pattern is actually like. Depending upon what exactly it is you would like to show and how many people you are observing, you can use one of several common methods of sampling. These are not rigid methods but examples of ways in which relatively fair sampling can be achieved. You will need to tailor the sampling method to your particular study.

Time sampling

If you are observing one child for the whole session you can decide on a suitable interval e.g. two minutes, then select two-minute intervals at random throughout the length of the appropriate session. In Orla's example it would be sensible to select these random periods during a free-play session but not during a story-telling activity. To select six two-minute sessions from a half-hour period at random you can divide the period into six sections (i.e. five minutes each) then select a random number from one to five, say three. You would then sample at three minutes, eight minutes and so on.

Point sampling

This refers to specific 'data points'. If you are observing several children, as Orla was, each is a 'point'. The order of observing these can be selected at random. This can be achieved by making a list of who will be observed and putting this list into an unpredictable sequence. For instance, if each child is to be observed three times in all, then make a list of names with each one repeated three times (e.g. James 1, James 2, James 3 and so on). Enter all these into a computer spreadsheet and ask the program to put the list in a random order. Follow this for your observations. Alternatively, make three lists of the children's names and randomly organise each one, then put the three lists themselves in random order. The intervals during which each child is observed can also be randomly selected as in the time sampling procedure described above.

Event sampling

Some events to be observed do not occur often enough to be included in procedures such as those just described. If you wanted, for instance, to observe how children find a place at story-telling time you might need to randomly sample several story-telling sessions, perhaps at several nurseries, in order to obtain adequate data.

PILOTING YOUR OBSERVATION PROCEDURES

It is extremely important that you *pilot* as much as possible of your proposed observation procedure. It is painful to organise a practical exercise, make all the necessary, usually lengthy, arrangements, go to gather data and then find that you cannot gather anything like sufficient data in the time available, or that there are too many things to observe, or that your checklist is inadequate for all the variations of behaviour you are witnessing. Very often observation opportunities cannot be repeated. Staff are too busy, too few children attend or your own time has run out.

Indirect observations

Your syllabus might permit you (but check first) to make indirect observations of human behaviour by using records or archives. These do not have to be formal records but simply records of human actions. For instance, consider the following:

- **personal advertisements in local newspapers**
- **formal advertisements on television and in print**
- **media interviews with stars, footballers, managers, etc.**
- **status of partners accompanying contestants in a game show**
- **types of jokes made by celebrities in panel games and quiz shows.**

CONTENT ANALYSIS

For these sorts of data, and in some cases for electronic recordings of behaviour, a system of content analysis can be used to categorise the data you have gathered. Usually you would first select a certain amount of sample information and use this to develop your categorisation system. For instance, if you wanted to analyse television advertisements for sex-role bias, you might observe a sample of prime time television advertisements and work out how these can be coded. You might classify the content of advertisements according to whether they depict: woman in active role; male as scientific expert; woman as homemaker; technical voice-over as male; female as alluring/feminine product; male as powerful/male product; and so on. Having developed your coding system you would now turn to a fair and representative selection of advertisements and use your coding system to record frequencies of each of the content categories that you have developed.

Research in Practice 19

Nigel investigated the differences between language used in personal advertisements in local papers by males and females. He initially developed categories of what was mentioned such as: long-term friendship; caring; fun; comical approach; action; etc.

He found that females used the categories of 'serious relationship', 'long-term friendship' and 'thinking about others' significantly more often than did males. They used the categories 'action', 'comical approach' and 'physical features' to a significantly less frequent extent.

Conclusion

Observations can be carried out where other approaches are not possible either for practical or for ethical reasons. Observations in the laboratory produce better control of distracting variables but do not lead to the collection of data on natural behaviour in an everyday setting. Observation studies require particular attention to definition of variables to be measured and to methods of sampling behaviour.

A B C D E F G H I J K L M N O P Q R S T U V W X Y Z

Describing your data

Creating a summary of your data

When you have finished data collection for your study you will have a set of raw data. This will be the scores of your participants or the frequencies of observations you have made, questionnaire responses and so on. You will need a summary of these in order to see whether the data fall into the pattern that you predicted. The raw data are *not* presented in the results section of your report but as an appendix. What you must do for yourself and for your reader is to *summarise* these data in an easily understandable form.

Decisions about your data

First, you must decide just what kind of variables you used in your study. You will have thought about this before you gathered them, but here you need to identify the type in order to choose the most appropriate descriptive procedure. The data will very often be summarised as measures of the dependent variable grouped in terms of the independent variable. For instance, let's return to the audience inhibition study introduced in Chapter 2. Suppose we had taken the following measures of dependent variables:

- **time in seconds to place all the pegs**
- **whether people dropped at least one peg or not**
- **the participants' rating of the difficulty of the task on a scale of 1 (easy) to 10 (hard).**

We need to summarise times, for instance, in terms of the 'alone' and 'presence' conditions. The first decision for each variable will be: was it categorical or measured?

CATEGORICAL VARIABLES PRODUCING NOMINAL LEVEL DATA

Time in seconds is a variable where, if we have a time for each person, we can *separate* scores along a line from high to low. Hence this variable is *measured*. However, whether each participant dropped a peg or not gives us merely a *categorical* variable – they either did or they didn't. This variable is said to produce *nominal level data*. The reason for this will become obvious if you have to enter your data into a statistical program such as SPSS. There you will have to code each person's response. You can't enter 'yes' (they did drop a peg) or 'no' they didn't. You will have to enter a number standing for yes and a number standing for no, say 1 and 2. However these numbers do not measure anything – they are simply labels or names – hence 'nominal'.

Other typical categorical variables producing nominal level data are:

- **whether participant is a full-time (1) or part-time (2) student**
- **whether people stopped (1) or didn't stop (2) at a traffic light**
- **whether a person did or didn't give 10 pence when asked**
- **whether a child chose a 'masculine' or 'feminine' toy**
- **whether a child said quantity had changed or hadn't changed**
- **whether a child chose an Afro-Caribbean (1), Asian (2) or White (3) doll as being 'like me'.**

Notice that we cannot find the average score for nominal level data. It would be meaningless to say that the mean score for stopping was 1.6 All we can do with this type of variable is to count frequencies – we can show how many people there were in each category.

RECOGNISING YOUR DATA AS CATEGORICAL OR MEASURED

The simplest thing to do is to ask, about each participant in your study, 'Did they have an individual score which is different from other people's scores and places them on a line between other people?' If so, you have a measured variable at ordinal level or above (see page 26). You could also ask: 'For each participant does my data on them place them in a category with several other people? *In* that category, if I ask no more questions, is there no distinction between the people in each category? (e.g. they are all vegetarians who are 'under 19'). If the answer to this is 'yes' then you have a categorical variable.

RECOGNISING YOUR DATA AS ORDINAL OR INTERVAL

You have used a *measured variable* if people's values on it can put them above or below other people with scores on that variable, even though there may be a few 'ties'. For instance consider the following typical values on a dependent variable:

- time (in seconds) to solve a problem
- rating of quality of a piece of writing – from 1 (poor) to 10 (excellent)
- number of words correctly recalled or identified
- score on an attitude scale or questionnaire
- number of times each child hit another (or spoke to, or looked at, etc.)
- estimates made by participants of their own IQ
- distance two people stand apart.

Chapter 4 discussed the nature of ordinal level and interval level data. The times people took to complete the peg-board task are measures at an interval level. Each unit of time is equal (e.g. seconds). To say that six seconds is twice three seconds makes sense. However, this does not make sense for the rating of difficulty variable. If I say I gave it an 8 and you gave it a 4 it is not safe to say I found it twice as difficult as you did since our estimates are entirely subjective. It is safe however to say that I found it harder than you did (though even this is debatable where people give similar values, e.g. 4 and 5).

As in the example just given, very often the data gathered in a psychological study *look* as though they are interval (because people can get different scores). However, if the scale is a human judgement scale and is invented, not standardised, then the data are best treated as ordinal level data. This means that you will eventually give ranks to the raw scores and your significance test will work on these ranks not the raw scores.

If the information you are gathering on each person is a countable quantity, such as number of words recalled correctly, or anagrams solved, then you are usually safe in treating these data as interval level as long as there is a large enough possible range of scores (e.g. 1 to 15 – which is a relatively small range).

DESCRIPTIVE STATISTICS

Having decided upon the appropriate level of measurement you are ready to **summarise** your *raw data* points into a meaningful, informative and fair presentation. For instance, was the female average for reading, as predicted, greater than the male average? Decisions made at this point are crucial. It is easy to hide embarrassing data and to emphasise those which support our case.

Categorical variables

If you have counted occurrences of different events you will want to present a table of *frequencies* such as that shown in Table 3.

Table 3 Frequency of aggressive actions observed

Type of aggressive behaviour	Hit	Push	Shout	Snatch object	Gesture	Other
Frequency	17	25	14	5	12	2

Note that in this kind of frequency table you can also identify a mode (see below). Here the modal category is 'Push'.

Very often you will have both a categorical independent variable and a categorical dependent variable. For instance, if you had asked people to lend you 10 pence dressed either shabbily or smartly you might obtain Table 5 shown on page 82. This is termed a 'Crosstabs' table. It shows the frequencies of one variable categorised by another. Here we have frequencies of donations and refusals categorised by the two conditions of the experiment.

Measured variables

If you have a set of scores to summarise then you will want to identify some form of 'average'. This will not be enough however because, for the same average, scores may be very much spread out around it or bunched very closely near it. Think of throwing darts at a point with your left and right hands. Though you might average around the same point with both hands the throws for one hand will usually range much more widely around that central point. These two types of descriptive statistic, average and spread, are known as measures of *central tendency* and of *dispersion*.

MEASURES OF CENTRAL TENDENCY

1 The mode

This is simply the most commonly occurring value. It is 8 in the data set below. A data set is the term for a group of values. Some data sets have more than one mode, where two values occur with equal frequency. The mode is useful where we have frequency data and wish to know what was the most 'popular' choice or most frequent value e.g. 'Who got the most medals at the Olympics?' or 'What number of children do most families have?'

Sample data set:

1 1 2 2 2 2 4 4 5 5 6 7 7 8 8 8 8 8 9 9 9 10 10

2 The median

The median is the mid-point of a set of data points and is appropriate where we have values organised in an ordinal manner. For instance the median in the set above is 7 (the central arrow). This is the 12ᵗʰ value in a set of 23, i.e. it is the central value when the values are placed in order. If we had an even number of data points – for instance 6, 8, 9, 12, 13, 14 – then the median is the mean of the two central values. In this set we have six values so the median is the 'sharing' of the two central values, the 3ʳᵈ and the 4ᵗʰ. These values are 9 and 12 so the median is the average of these: (9 + 12)/2 and this gives us 21/2 = 10.5

Note: the median is not affected by large 'rogue' scores. If the last value in the sample data set above were 100 instead of 10, the median would stay the same, still giving us a fair impression of the central trend in the set.

3 The mean

This will be by far the most common central tendency measure you will meet, but do remember that the median is more appropriate for ordinal level data. However, with most psychological scales, standardised or not, it is usually acceptable to present the mean of the set.

The mean of the set above is 5.9 – this is found by adding all the scores and then dividing by the number of scores there are in the set. The formula for this is:

$$\bar{x} = \frac{\sum x}{N}$$

$\bar{x}$ is the symbol for the mean and it is found by adding up all your scores then dividing by the number (N) you had of them. The sum of the numbers above is 135 so the mean is 135/23 which is 5.9.

Notes: the mean could be reported as 5.8696 here but this would be ludicrous. We only measured originally to the nearest whole number so the appropriate number of decimal places is one more than this, i.e. one place. Any further places give an impression of 'spurious accuracy' – accuracy that can't actually be claimed for the original measure. Beware of this when copying from a calculator or computer program.

Only report one central tendency

You should always select the measure of central tendency that is most suitable for your level of data measurement. You should not report the mean, median and the mode in your results section (unless instructed to do so for teaching purposes). This is not necessary. The information is redundant. One central tendency measure is sufficient, and usually only one is appropriate.

MEASURES OF DISPERSION

These are measures of the spread of the data around the central tendency.

The range

Our simplest measure of dispersion is simply to give the spread of scores from top to bottom.

The *range* is: **(top score – bottom score) + 1**

The 1 is added to allow for measurement limits. When we report heights in whole *inches*, e.g. 5′ 4″, we are actually saying that the person is somewhere between 5′ 3½″ and 5′ 4½″ tall. We are measuring to the nearest *inch*. Hence the difference between 5′ 3″ and 5′ 8″ could be as great as 6″ (5′ 2½″ to 5′ 8½″) and the range gives us this maximum distance.

Semi-interquartile range

The range does not tell us anything about the variation between top and bottom scores. Instead of just looking at the extremes we can get a better idea of the spread of our scores by looking at how they are arranged around the measure of central tendency. Where this measure is the median it is appropriate to look at the quartiles around that median position. *Quartiles* are a division of a data set into quarters when they are arranged from lowest to highest. The quartiles for the sample data set shown above are indicated by arrows at the 6th, 12th and 18th positions in the set.

We are interested in the distance between the 1st and 3rd quartiles. This is 8 – 2 and = 6. This is the *inter-quartile range*. The *semi-interquartile range* is half of this value so 6/2 = 3 and the formula is:

$$\frac{Q_3 - Q_1}{2}$$

THE STANDARD DEVIATION

Where we are using an interval measure it is appropriate to use the *standard deviation* or *variance*. With large data sets the standard deviation will tell us the point above and below the means where roughly 68 per cent of all values lie. The formula to use is:

$$s = \sqrt{\frac{\sum(x - \bar{x})^2}{N - 1}}$$

To calculate the standard deviation of the data set above:

1   Find the mean – this is 5.9 as we saw above.

2   Find each score's deviation from the mean. A deviation score is simply how far a score is from the mean. A score of 7 here will obtain a deviation score of:

$$7 - 5.9 = 1.1$$

The formula for a deviation score is $x - \bar{x}$. A score of 4 would obtain:

$$4 - 5.9 = -1.9$$

(note the negative sign).

3   Square each deviation score (the negative signs now disappear).

4   Add up all the squared deviations.

5   Divide the result by $N - 1$ (this is the variance 8.93).

6   Find the square root of step 5 – this is the standard deviation (2.99).

Note: The use of $N - 1$ in the formula is a 'correction factor' because the standard deviation and variance are usually used as estimates of the population parameters from the sample statistics. Where only the standard deviation of a group is required, the –1 can be dropped but this is rarely done so best to stick to the $N - 1$ form in your practical work.

Inferential statistics – testing for significance

Having described your data and having found that there was a difference or a correlation in the direction that you predicted, the next step is to conduct a test of statistical significance. When testing the difference between two samples for significance it is important to remember that we are assuming that the samples we have taken are representative of the populations from which they were drawn. Our significance test is about these populations and not about the specific samples we have. We are using the samples to gauge whether there is a real difference between the populations. To do this we take the following steps:

1 **Assume that the null hypothesis (H_0) is true. This is (often) the hypothesis that the two populations are equal (or at least that their means are equal). It is therefore assumed that any observed variation between samples is entirely the result of random sampling error.**

2 **Find the probability that the observed difference would occur *If H_0* is true.**

3 **If this probability is less than 0.05 then reject H_0 and accept the alternative hypothesis.**

How do we find the probability of these results occurring if the null hypothesis is true?

1 **Choose an appropriate statistical test – see page 80.**

2 **Calculate the test statistic (e.g. *t, U,* etc. (Note that every statistical test has an associated symbol.)**

3 **Check the obtained value of the test statistic (i.e. yours) against the critical value found in tables for *N* or *df*, and for either a one- or two-tailed test as appropriate.**

A one-tailed test *may* be used where your hypothesis is directional, that is, you state which population scores are higher (e.g. females score higher than males). However, many statisticians would argue that psychological research studies can rarely, if ever, make use of one-tailed tests – see Coolican, 1999 for further detail. If your hypothesis does not state a direction, or just to be statistically safe, use a two-tailed test. Using a one- or two-tailed test simply means using a different part of the critical value table when you check your test statistic.

Choosing an appropriate statistical test

To choose the appropriate significance test to use on your data, using Table 4, you need to answer the following questions in this order.

1 Difference or correlation?
   Are you looking for a difference between samples of scores or for a correlation between pairs of scores, one on each of two measured variables?

2 Level of data measurement – categorical or measured?
   For differences, you need to decide whether your data are categorical or measured. If they are in categorical form (frequency counts in categories) then treat them as nominal level data.

   If they are measured variables you have to decide whether to treat them as interval level data or whether to play safe and reduce them to ordinal level data (by ranking them). For correlations you have to make the decision just described between interval and ordinal level treatment of data.

3 Type of design – related or unrelated data?
   For differences you also need to decide whether the research design for these particular data is related or unrelated. Do you have two *related* sets of data where each score in one set is paired specifically with a score in the other set? This will happen where participants have performed the *same* task under different conditions (repeated measures) or where matched and paired participants have each performed the same task but in two different conditions. If you have a set of scores from one group of people and another set of scores from a separate and unmatched group of people, then you have *unrelated* data (gathered from studies with an independent samples design).

Having made these three decisions you should be able to isolate the specific test appropriate for your data. For instance, one version of Judy's tail-fin study (see Research in Practice 14, page 28), looked for *differences* between extroverts and introverts (*unrelated* groups) on rating of fins. This rating is an invented, not standardised, measure hence the data might be treated at an *ordinal* level and therefore a Mann–Whitney test would be chosen.

Table 4 Choosing the appropriate significance test for your data

Nature of hypothesis test:	Level of measurement of test data:	Type of research design: Unrelated	Related
Differences	Categorical variable: *nominal level data*	chi-square	sign test
	Measured variable: *ordinal level data*	Mann–Whitney	Wilcoxon (matched pairs)
	Interval level data	independent *t* test	related *t* test
Correlation	*ordinal level data*		Spearman ρ
	interval level data		Pearson *r*

Tests of difference

CHI-SQUARE (χ^2)

Type of design: **Unrelated** (independent samples; between groups)

Type of data: **Frequencies**; categorical data

Hypothesis: **Difference** between population distributions or association between variables

Typical data source

Sarah's practical group asked students in the refectory whether they would help her by giving her a 10 pence piece for the phone. In one condition she wore smart clothing and in the other she was dressed rather shabbily. The quasi-experiment took rather longer than they thought and they were only able to gather the data shown in Table 5.

Table 5 People giving and not giving 10 pence when requested by a shabbily and a smartly dressed stranger

Observed frequencies	Type of dress		
	Smart	**Shabby**	**Total**
10 pence not given	a 1	b 9	10
10 pence given	c 6	d 4	10
Total:	7	13	20

To calculate chi-square (χ^2)

1   Call the gathered data the 'observed frequencies' (O)

2   Create a table of 'expected frequencies' (E) as follows:

   i For each cell, labelled 'a', 'b', 'c', 'd', above, calculate R × C/T. That is, row total (R) multiplied by column total (C) and divided by overall total (T)

   ii Put the calculated expected value into a new table as shown below.

Table 6 Calculated expected frequencies

Expected frequencies	Type of dress		
	Smart	**Shabby**	**Total**
10 pence not given	3.5	6.5	10
10 pence given	3.5	6.5	10
Total:	7	13	20

3   Calculate chi-square, cell by cell, using:

$$\chi^2 = \sum \frac{(O - E)^2}{E}$$

This gives: $\dfrac{(1 - 3.5)^2}{3.5} + \dfrac{(9 - 6.5)^2}{6.5} + \dfrac{(6 - 3.5)^2}{3.5} + \dfrac{(4 - 6.5)^2}{6.5} =$

$1.786 + 0.961 + 1.786 + 0.961 = \mathbf{5.494}$

4 Find the appropriate number of 'degrees of freedom' (*df*) using $(R - 1) \times (C - 1) = 1$

5 Check this obtained value for chi-square (5.494) against the critical value found in Table A3 for $p < 0.05$. Chi-square must always be calculated as a two-tailed test. For 1 *df* and a two-tailed test you should find that the critical value we need to exceed in order to claim a significant difference here is 3.84. Our obtained value of 5.494 exceeds this value so our difference is significant and we reject the null hypothesis. The null hypothesis here would state that the population of frequencies, from which this sample was obtained, is arranged as are the expected frequencies. In other words, in the population, there is no difference between the 'smart' and 'shabby' frequencies of giving 10 pence. Our result casts doubt on this proposal.

Notes

1 **Unrelated frequencies**
   The frequencies in the chi-square cells must be unrelated and independent. For instance, in Table 7 the data break this rule and cannot be used in a chi-square analysis, because a particular mother or father could appear in both the 'son' and 'daughter' cells:

2 **Frequencies only!**

Table 7 Data unsuitable
for chi-square analysis

Table 8 Low count example

	Would hit:			Handedness:	
	Son	**Daughter**		**Left**	**Right**
Mother	23	36	Dyslexic	2	27
Father	35	14	Non-dyslexic	2	94

Only unrelated frequencies can be analysed by chi-square. The data in the cells cannot be ratios, proportions, means, etc. They can only be frequencies – one entry for each case. That is, each person goes in only one cell and once only. You cannot enter several results (e.g. choices; stimuli detected) for each person in one cell.

A B C D E F G H I J K L M N O P Q R S T U V W X Y Z

3   Low expected frequencies

Try not to use a design which is likely to produce data where there are very few instances in one or more of the cells. For instance, anything to do with left and right handedness is likely to produce low counts – see Table 8. As a general rule of thumb, chi-square results are unreliable if more than 20 per cent of expected frequency cells are below 5.

One solution to low frequencies, sometimes possible, is to merge columns or rows. In the table below the vegans can be merged into the vegetarian column giving the frequencies shown on the right.

Table 9 Unmerged columns

	Meat eater	Vegetarian	Vegan
Pro-hunting	35	12	0
Anti-hunting	27	51	3

Table 10 Merged columns from Table 9

	Meat eater	Vegetarian
Pro-hunting	35	12
Anti-hunting	27	54

THE SIGN TEST (*S*)

Type of design: **Related** (repeated measures; matched pairs; within groups)
Type of data: **Frequencies** – yes/no, plus/minus for each case
Hypothesis: **Difference** between frequencies of signs in population

Typical data source

Jason was permitted to visit a mother and baby club where he showed babies of around four months old two pictures of a face, one smiling and one not. He displayed each face alternately for five seconds, changing the initial order for different children, and recorded which of the two stimuli was the first that the baby smiled at. In the results table he recorded a '+' for those babies who smiled at the smiling face first, and a '–' for those who smiled at the non-smiling face first.

Table 11 Babies' first smiling response ('+' to smiling face; '–' to non-smiling face)

Baby No:	1	2	3	4	5	6	7	8	9	10	11	12
Result:	+	+	+	–	+	+	–	+	+	+	+	+

'+' = first smile to smiling face = 10
'–' = first smile to non-smiling face = 2

To calculate the sign test (S)

1 Simply count up the number of less frequently occurring signs (i.e. those cases that 'went the wrong way'). The total is 2. Call this value S.

2 Find the critical value of S from Table A8 using N, the total number of results, one- or two-tailed values and $p < 0.05$. The obtained S must be equal to or less than the critical value. Here, for a two-tailed test, the critical value for $N = 12$ with $p < 0.05$ is 2.

Hence this difference can be counted as significant and Jason may reject the null hypothesis that there are equal numbers of '+' and '−' results in the overall population of results. He can claim support for the hypothesis that babies of four months smile more readily to (and can therefore recognise) a smiling face.

Notes

The sign test can also be used in a related design that gathered two scores for each participant on an interval or ordinal level of measurement. For instance, we might have 'number of words correctly recalled by each participant under two conditions, one in silence and the other with loud background noise'. We could record that participants either improved (+) or worsened (−) under noise conditions. However, here we would usually prefer to use the Wilcoxon signed ranks test or the related t test (see below) since these tests make more use of the available information in the data. The scores tell us *how much* a participant was better or worse. The sign test only tells us that they *were* better or worse. The Wilcoxon and t tests are more likely to show significance for the same set of data.

If you *do* use differences between scores, and record each as a '+' or a '−', then you will have to completely discount any results giving a difference of zero. N does not include these zeros and is only the sum of the + and − signs.

THE MANN–WHITNEY U TEST

Type of design: **Unrelated** (independent samples; between groups)
Type of data: **Ordinal** ranks or scores that have been ranked
Hypothesis: **Difference** between (medians of) populations of scores

Typical data source

Rajinder asked students to watch a five-minute video interview of another student answering simple questions about her lifestyle, job, relationships, likes and dislikes, etc. One group were told this was the beginning of a job interview while a second group were told that the woman had approached the interviewer for mental health support. Students used a checklist of 'mental illness symptoms' to score the woman's behaviour (out of 100) during the interview. The data gathered are shown in Table 12, first and third columns below.

To calculate the Mann–Whitney *U* test

1   Arrange your data as shown in Table 12. Here the scores for each group are listed in columns in ascending order.

2   Allocate points to each score as follows:

Table 12 Mental health symptom scores out of 100 given when interviewee is 'job applicant' and 'seeking mental health support'

Job interview Group A score	Points	Mental health support Group B score	Points
17	10	23	8
22	10	28	5.5
27	9	30	3
27	9	31	2
28	8.5	41	1
29	8	48	1
29	8	55	1
31	6.5	78	0
31	6.5	80	0
77	3	89	0
Total:	78.5		21.5

Table 13 Data from Table 12 ranked for use with formula version of Mann–Whitney

Job interview Group A	Rank	Mental health support Group B	Rank
17	1	23	3
22	2	28	6.5
27	4.5	30	10
27	4.5	31	12
28	6.5	41	14
29	8.5	48	15
29	8.5	55	16
31	12	78	18
31	12	80	19
77	17	89	20
$R_A =$	76.5	$R_B =$	133.5

   i 1 point for every higher score in the other group (e.g. there are 10 scores in Group B above 17 in Group A)

   ii half a point for every score in the other group which shares its position (e.g. there are five scores in Group A higher than the 28 in Group B and one score *at* 28).

3   Add the points for each group. The lower of these is Mann–Whitney U.

4   Call the number of scores in Group A 'N_a' and the number of scores in Group B 'N_b'.

5   Check the critical value for U in Table A2 for N_a and N_b. Here, for a two-tailed test and $N_a = 10$ and $N_b = 10$, U must be equal to or less than 23 for significance. Hence, because our obtained U is 21.5, these two groups differ significantly and we may reject H_0.

Notes

Where it is obvious (as in most cases) which group will have the smaller points (i.e. the group with the higher scores) there is no need to allocate points for the other group. In the example above we needed only to allocate points for Group B.

Most texts give formulae for calculating U as follows:

$$U_A = N_A N_A + \frac{N_A(N_A + 1)}{2} - R_A \qquad U_B = N_B N_B + \frac{N_B(N_B + 1)}{2} - R_B$$

N_A is the number in the first group and N_B is the number in the second. R_A and R_B are the sums of ranks of scores in each group when all the scores are ranked together, as in Table 13. U is the smaller of U_A and U_B.

However, where numbers of participants are relatively small (e.g. 15 in each group) you'll probably find the points method a lot easier than the formulae.

WILCOXON MATCHED PAIRS SIGNED RANKS (T)

Type of design: **Related** (repeated measures; matched pairs; within groups)
Type of data: **Ordinal** – ranks or scores that have been ranked
Hypothesis: **Difference** between (medians of) populations of scores

The wordy title is needed because there is another Wilcoxon test for unrelated designs. The T is upper case and you should be careful not to confuse this with the little t used for interval level tests in the next section.

Typical data source

Alex asked ten students to rate their attitude to physical punishment on a scale of 1 to 20 where 20 indicated strongly in favour. He made the same measurement again after all the students had engaged in a debate on physical punishment. He reasoned that attitudes should move against physical punishment as the students were exposed to negative information which they probably had not heard before.

Table 14 Attitudes to physical punishment before and after a debate on the issue, measured from 1 (= strongly against) to 20 (strongly in favour)

Before debate	After debate	Difference	Rank
9	2	7	7.5
19	12	7	7.5
7	9	-2	3
7	7	0	

Before debate	After debate	Difference	Rank
7	8	−1	*1.5*
6	1	5	5
16	15	1	1.5
12	9	3	4
17	11	6	6
13	5	8	9

To calculate Wilcoxon's *T*

1 Find the difference between each pair of scores, always subtracting in the same direction.

2 Rank these differences, ignoring the sign. Exclude from the analysis any cases with a difference of zero.

3 Add the ranks of the positive and negative differences (add only the smaller group if this is obvious – italicised in the table above)

4 This smaller sum of ranks is *T*. In this case *T* is 4.5.

5 Check *T* in Table A1. In this case, for a two-tailed test, with $N = 9$, *T* must be ≤ 5 for significance with $p < 0.05$. The difference is therefore significant.

THE *T* TEST FOR RELATED SAMPLES

Type of design: **Related** (repeated measures; matched pairs; within groups)

Type of data: **Interval** – scores on a scale with equal intervals

Hypothesis: **Difference** between means of score populations

This tests the difference between the means of your two samples for significance. Use this test when you can be sure that your data are gathered on an interval scale. Included in this category would be physical measures (such as length in cm, time), countable items (such as number of words correctly recalled) and measures on standardised psychological scales. This applies to most published scales (e.g. Eysenck's EPQ; The British Ability Scales). If the data are obviously skewed (i.e. do not spread out in a similar formation to a normal distribution), use Wilcoxon's test, see above.

Typical data source

Rowena has tested participants on a needle-threading task under two conditions, one with an observing audience present and one without an audience. The times taken to thread the needle are shown below.

Table 15 Time taken to thread a needle, in seconds, before an audience and alone

Time to thread needle in condition:		Difference between conditions (a–b)
Audience (a)	Alone (b)	
27	24	3
24	12	12
35	23	12
18	16	2
25	28	−3
36	24	12
49	34	15
35	15	20
24	22	2
16	24	−8

Mean difference = 6.7

Standard deviation of differences = 8.81

To calculate related *t* test

1 Find the difference between each pair of scores.

2 Find the mean ($\bar{d}$) and standard deviation (S_d) of these differences.

3 Use these in the formula:

$$t = \frac{\bar{d}}{S_d/\sqrt{N}} = \frac{6.7}{8.81/\sqrt{10}} = 2.40$$

4 Check the obtained value of *t* against critical values in Table A4, where *df* are *N* – 1. *t* must be equal to or greater than the critical value for significance.

For a two-tailed test with $df = 9$ and $p < 0.05$, critical value is 2.26. Hence the difference is significant.

THE *T* TEST FOR UNRELATED SAMPLES

Type of design: **Unrelated** (independent samples; between groups)
Type of data: **Interval** – scores on a scale with equal intervals
Hypothesis: **Difference** between means of score populations

See the notes about the related *t* test, above, concerning interval level of data measurement and the fit to a normal distribution. In addition, if you have quite unequal numbers in your two samples, and the variances of the two groups of scores are very different, it is safer to use the Mann–Whitney test.

Typical data source

Nastasia conducted a study in which she asked a control group to learn a list of words and then attempt recall after five minutes on a different task. She asked the experimental group to learn the words but they had to move to a different room for their recall session. She predicted that the control group would recall more words since their learning context was the same as their recall context. The data she obtained are shown in Table 16.

Table 16 Number of words correctly recalled in same and different recall contexts

Recall in:	
Same room (a)	Different room (b)
12	12
18	9
12	12
10	8
10	10
14	8
14	7
18	13
12	16
8	11
14	15
14	13
	9

To calculate unrelated *t* test

Find the following values: Values for Table 16

$\bar{x}_a$	= The mean of the scores in column a	13
$\bar{x}_b$	= The mean of the scores in column b	11
Σx_a	= The sum of all the scores in column a	156
Σx_b	= The sum of all the scores in column b	143
Σx_a^2	= The sum of the squares of all the x_a values	2128
Σx_b^2	= The sum of the squares of all the x_b values	1667
$(\Sigma x_a)^2$	= The square of the sum of the x_a scores	24336
$(\Sigma x_b)^2$	= The square of the sum of the x_b scores	20449
df	$= N_a + N_b - 2$	23

Be very careful to distinguish between Σx_a^2 and $(\Sigma x_a)^2$. In the first you square each x_a score then add up the results. In the second you add all the x_a scores then square the result. The two answers are very different indeed!

Put all these values into the equation:

$$t = \frac{|\bar{x}_a - \bar{x}_b|}{\sqrt{\left[\dfrac{\left(\Sigma x_a^2 - \dfrac{(\Sigma x_a)^2}{N_a}\right) + \left(\Sigma x_b^2 - \dfrac{(\Sigma x_b)^2}{N_b}\right)}{(N_a + N_b - 2)}\right]\left[\dfrac{N_a + N_b}{(N_a)(N_b)}\right]}}$$

Yes! Compared with all the others so far this one is nasty. However, don't panic. Simply slot every separate value that you have calculated into its respective place then run through the calculations step by step making a record all the time of just where you have got to.

You should get a *t* of **1.72**. Check this against the critical value found in Table A4. For a two-tailed test with 23 *df* and for $p < 0.05$, *t* must be equal to or greater than the critical value of **2.069.** It isn't. It just scrapes above the critical value for a one-tailed test (**1.714**).

Note

The value on the top of the formula above $|\bar{x}_a - \bar{x}_b|$ is simply the difference between the two means taken as positive. That is if you get a negative value, simply discard the negative sign.

TESTS OF CORRELATION: PEARSON'S CORRELATION (r)

Type of design: **Related** (repeated measures; matched pairs)
Type of data: **Interval** – scores on a scale with equal intervals
Hypothesis: **Correlation** in the population from which sample taken

Use this when you have two scores for each participant and you want to see whether there is a significant correlation between these two sets of scores.

Typical data source

Kiran has assessed people's verbal and numerical abilities using two standardised tests with a maximum score of 20. She proposes that the scores will correlate since she is testing the theory that they are both aspects of a more general intellectual ability. The raw data appear below.

Table 17 Scores on verbal and numerical ability given out of a maximum of 20

Verbal score (x)	$x - \bar{x} = d_x$	Numerical score (y)	$y - \bar{y} = d_y$	$d_x \times d_y$
6	−5.33	7	−6.08	32.41
18	6.67	15	1.92	12.81
5	−6.33	15	1.92	−12.15
13	1.67	12	−1.08	−1.80
7	−4.33	18	4.92	−21.30
2	−9.33	3	−10.08	94.04
19	7.67	18	4.92	37.74
15	3.67	16	2.92	10.72
14	2.67	16	2.92	7.80
15	3.67	14	0.92	3.38
13	1.67	13	−0.08	−0.13
9	−2.33	10	−3.08	7.18
$\bar{x} = 11.3$		$\bar{y} = 13.08$	$\Sigma(d_x \times d_y) =$	170.7
$S_x = 5.42$		$S_y = 4.50$		

To calculate Pearson's r

The scores for each participant on the two scales are shown in columns 1 and 3 of Table 17.

1   Find the mean and standard deviation of each set of scores. That's $\bar{x}$, $\bar{y}$, S_x and S_y shown at the bottom of the columns.

2   Take the mean from each score – see columns 2 and 4. This gives $x - \bar{x}$ (which we'll call d_x) and $y - \bar{y}$ (or d_y).

3   Multiply each d_x by each d_y.

4   Add up all the results of Step 3. That is, find $\Sigma(d_x \times d_y)$.

5   Put this value into the top line of the formula below to find r:

$$r = \frac{\Sigma(x - \bar{x})(y - \bar{y})}{(N - 1)S_x S_y}$$

6   Find $df = N - 2$

7   Check r against the critical value found in Table A6. For a two-tailed test with 10 df, for significance with $p < 0.05$ r must be ≥ 0.576.

$$r = \frac{170.7}{11 \times 5.42 \times 4.50} = 0.636$$

In the example above, then, the r of 0.636 is significant with $p < 0.05$.

TESTS OF CORRELATION: SPEARMAN'S RANK CORRELATION (ρ = 'RHO')

Type of design: **Related** (repeated measures; matched pairs)
Type of data: **Ordinal** – ranks, or scores that have been ranked
Hypothesis: **Correlation** in the population from which sample taken

Katrina has assessed attitudes on two invented scales, one concerning physical punishment of children and one concerning treatment of criminals and prisoners. Testing the theory that attitudes to specific issues are related by a deeper, more general personality characteristic, Katrina hypothesises that attitudes to children – from disciplinarian to liberal – will be related to a similar position for offender treatment. The raw data appear in Table 18.

To calculate Spearman's rho

1   Rank all the scores in each group separately. Spearman's rho is actually a Pearson's r carried out on these two sets of ranks. However, the following is a quick estimate formula as long as there are not too many tied ranks (see Note below).

2 Find the difference between each pair of ranks (d).

3 Square each d ($= d^2$).

4 Find the sum of d^2 and use this in the formula:

$$\rho = 1 - \frac{6\Sigma d^2}{N(N^2 - 1)}$$

5 Use $N - 1$ df to check for significance.

In the example above:

$$\rho = \frac{6 \times 81}{10(100 - 1)} = \frac{486}{990} = 0.491$$

which is compared with the Table A5 critical value of 0.618 for a two-tailed test with $p < 0.05$. The correlation is *not* significant (nor would it be for a one-tailed test).

Table 18 Attitudes to physical punishment (PP) and offender treatment (OT)

Attitude to Physical punishment PP	Rank of PP	Attitude to offender treatment OT	Rank of OT	Diff between ranks d	d^2
8	9	9	10	−1	1
7	7.5	6	7	0.5	0.25
9	10	5	3.5	6.5	42.25
5	4	6	7	−3	9
6	5.5	5	3.5	2	4
3	2	5	3.5	−1.5	2.25
4	3	6	7	−4	16
2	1	4	1	0	0
6	5.5	5	3.5	2	4
7	7.5	8	9	−1.5	2.25
			$\Sigma d^2 =$		81

Notes

If ρ or rho has a negative value then this is a *negative correlation*, e.g. high score on punishment and low score on offender attitude and vice versa. A two-tailed test would still give significance but a one-tailed cannot, since the outcome would be the opposite of what was predicted.

The issue of ties is not problematic for most student projects unless the measurement scale used creates large numbers of identical scores (e.g. where participants can only score 1, 2 or 3).

Writing your practical report

The first rule about writing your report is:

don't put it off!

If you leave the write-up until long after you conducted the study you'll find it difficult to pick up the threads of what you did and you're likely to miss important details of why you used certain procedures, what exactly went wrong with the study, what could be improved, etc. Your class colleagues may no longer have their data and may well be too busy to help you with information.

Why are you writing a report?

Apart from the obvious fact that your syllabus requires it, there are several good reasons for writing a report.

1 This is how psychological knowledge develops. Psychological researchers conduct studies, write them up, get them published and can then read about each other's work in a number of journals dedicated to different aspects of psychology. Knowledge is also disseminated at specialist conferences but here too, psychologists must write and present a 'paper' looking very much like the report that you must write.

2 This is the way that you tell readers how they could replicate your work if they want to. This is a central feature of scientific activity – the replication of new work to see whether other researchers can obtain the same results. If they can, the psychological effect looks sound. If they can't, there may well be something wrong with the original research or it might only 'work' in the particular context in which it was originally conducted.

If you always keep point 2 in mind, and write up your work accordingly, you cannot fail to get good marks for your report.

Think from the reader's point of view at all times.

If they can understand and easily replicate your work, then you have written a good report. Before you hand in a report, read it out to yourself aloud, or give it to a friend to read. Make sure that it all makes sense to them and that they could repeat exactly what you did. Don't say 'But it's OK the reader would be a psychologist so they'd understand.' The reader was not with you and does not know exactly what you did.

A NOTE ON PLAGIARISM

One thing you simply must avoid in writing up a report, as in writing an essay, is plagiarism. This means the direct copying of another person's words, without recognition of your source, or the copying of a line of argument without recognition, even *if* you use different words to outline the argument. For instance, if you are writing about social facilitation and you 'lift' a few paragraphs from your favourite psychology textbook and put them into your own report, without using quotation marks and stating where the quotation comes from, that is direct plagiarism and is very much frowned upon in academic circles. It is basically stealing another person's work. In the same way, if your textbook contains a series of statements in an argument about how schemas affect the reconstruction of events in our memory, then, if you use exactly the same steps of argument, you should attribute your source, even if you use your own words in each step of the argument. Here you are not stealing the exact words but stealing the thought patterns of another author.

Students often claim that they didn't realise they were plagiarising. They had their textbook open, copied out certain sections, then, later, didn't realise they were not their own words taken as notes whilst they were reading their textbook. Apart from the implausibility of this story (you can usually spot the difference between your own writing style and that of a textbook author!), this excuse just will not do since, *intentional or not*, copying other people's work is plagiarism.

How should my report be set out?

The box on the next page gives the set of headings you'll need for a conventional report. If your report is qualitative then you might find that you are advised by your tutor to merge the results and discussion section. Otherwise, the report should contain exactly the same sections.

A B C D E F G H I J K L M N O P Q R S T U V W X Y Z

Projects in Practice

Sections of a conventional psychology practical report

Title

Abstract

Introduction

Method

  Design

  Participants

  Materials/apparatus

  Procedure

Results

  Descriptive findings

  Treatment/Analysis

Discussion

References

Appendices

GENERAL DOS AND DON'TS ABOUT YOUR REPORT

Do

- Number each page.

- Carry the text on from section to section.

- Number and title each table and figure (e.g. chart).

- Put raw data, calculations, sets of stimuli, questionnaires, etc. into the appendix.

- Make sure that all references made in your text are included in the reference section.

Don't

- Waste valuable time and effort on artistic detail. You won't gain any extra points for beautifully drawn diagrams, inclusion of amusing clipart or coloured, shaped lettering for your title.

- Leave almost a side of blank paper because it is the end of the introduction. Carry straight on with the method section.

- Include raw data in the results section.

The title

This should be a concise statement of the effect you investigated. You don't really need to state the exact design here so:

> Card sorting with and without the presence of an audience

is a good title and far preferable to:

> An experiment to see whether people sort cards faster or slower when an audience is watching them compared to when they are working alone.

In conventional studies the title is a statement of the proposed link between the variables in the study, for instance:

> The effect of sunny or cloudy weather on donation to a street beggar

> The relationship between extroversion/introversion and attitude to sport

> The difference between students' and truck drivers' attitudes to the environment.

Abstract

Your abstract (also known as a 'Summary') is a very brief description of the central features of your study. Good abstract writing is a very sophisticated skill and you are not expected to be perfect. However, the single criterion here is to pare down detail to the absolutely essential in order to appreciate what your study was about and what happened. A good abstract will contain only:

- the context (brief reference to relevant theory being explored)

- the main variables, especially the independent variable and dependent variable

- the participants – who was studied?

- the design – how was the research conducted (e.g. was it an experiment? If so what kind? If it was an observation study, what type?)

- the results – no detail, just the main effects (or lack of them)

- the conclusion (and possibly some comment on a major flaw).

All this can and ought to be achieved in just a few sentences, perhaps only four. For example:

Projects in Practice

Audience effects on a decision-making task were investigated in a repeated measures experiment by asking 26 male and female college students to sort animal pictures into given categories under two conditions, one whilst alone and the other whilst in the presence of an audience of six other students. Participants sorted faster in the alone condition than in the audience condition and this difference was significant. However, the numbers of errors made in the two conditions did not differ significantly. The result fails to support the cognitive–motivational model of social facilitation proposed by Paulus (1983) which would predict more errors in the audience condition for a complex task.

This abstract contains 108 words and just four sentences, yet it completes all the tasks listed above. The idea of an abstract is that it contains enough information for a reader to decide that they ought to read further or whether they can go on to read other abstracts that might contain work of greater relevance to their own research.

The introduction

The introduction contains three major elements:

* **background literature of relevance**
* **rationale for the present study**
* **statement of aims and/or hypothesis/hypotheses.**

The background literature need not be extensive, just relevant to the topic under study. You should not write here a mini-essay of the 'All I could find concerning ...' type (see also page 7). You need only include the studies and theories that help a naïve reader understand just why the research was conducted and what its overall aims and predictions were. An example is given below.

Projects in Practice
Introduction to a study on conservation

Piaget (1963) argued that children pass through qualitatively different stages of cognitive development. Each of these depends upon the child having mastered certain types of cognitive operation. In the pre-operational stage of development, according to Piaget, children are unable to 'conserve' features of the physical world. They do not see that, although the superficial features of an object might change, its fundamental characteristics stay the same so long as nothing has been added or taken away. For instance, a ball of clay retains the same mass and volume even though it may change to a sausage shape. Piaget showed that children in the pre-operational stage (lasting roughly between 2 and 7 years old) tended to judge that a taller thinner glass contained more orange juice than a shorter fatter glass when they had previously agreed that two short fat glasses had exactly the same amount of juice in them. The juice from one short fat glass had then been poured into the taller thinner glass. Piaget argued that the children could not 'decentre'. That is, they could not stop themselves centring on one aspect of the situation, the height of the juice in the glass, and therefore ignoring another aspect, its width. They also could not move away from the physical looks and judge according to the abstract 'conservation' principle that nothing added or taken away means that quantities must stay the same.

Piaget's claims that children as old as 7 were unable to decentre and to conserve were challenged by many researchers. One group argued that when the adult changes the arrangement of things in the child's view, then asks a second identical question, it could be that children assume something must have changed. McGarrigle and Donaldson (1974) showed that older children could conserve number when a 'Naughty Teddy' rearranged counters rather than the adult investigator. To demonstrate conservation of number this procedure involves laying out two rows of counters, say black and white, so that each black counter is clearly opposite a white counter. When the adult stretches out the line of

Continued

black counters at either end the child tends to say that there are more black counters present. However, when 'Naughty Teddy' swooped down and moved the black counters, far more children said there were still as many white as black counters. Here the change is accidental and the second question appears to be asked for good reason. Fewer children seem to assume that the adult expects a different answer to their second question.

Rose and Blank (1974) avoided the problem of asking a second identical question, after altering the counters, by removing the first question altogether. They showed children the counters in one-to-one correspondence, then stretched out one row and only then asked if there was the same number of counters in each row. Far more six year olds were able to answer correctly here than in the standard two-question task. Samuel and Bryant (1984) confirmed these findings, using this technique, for number, quantity and liquid volume (Gross, 1996).

Our study uses this technique but we used solid volume. That is we used the classic Playdo version in which the child sees two identical balls of Playdo, then one ball is rolled out into a sausage shape. At this point we asked the single question which required the child to say whether each lump of Playdo had the same amount in it or not.

We wanted to compare performance with the standard procedure so we used pairs of children from a reception class and paired these on their current numeracy ability, randomly allocating one to the standard procedure and one to the single-question procedure.

We predicted that more children in the single-question condition than in the standard two-question condition would correctly answer that the two lumps contained the same amount of Playdo.

Note that this does not take the reader through the entire breadth of Piaget's developmental stages, nor through dozens of irrelevant but interesting empirical studies related to other aspects of Piaget's claims about cognitive development. It starts in at the central concept involved in the hypothesis under test – the meaning of conservation and the suggestion that children do not conserve until around seven years old. It then examines one or two relevant critical studies and the main points that these were making. Finally, it presents a 'rationale'. This is an argument that takes the reader through the reasoning that leads up to the hypothesis to be tested and the specific predictions you are making for the outcome of your study. Finally a precise research prediction is given. The general hypothesis tested is that the single-question procedure produces more correct answers to the conservation question. You can state this form of general hypothesis or give the exact prediction for the study. Either counts as 'stating your hypothesis'.

STATING THE HYPOTHESIS PRECISELY – A CRUCIAL ELEMENT IN REPORTS

However, your prediction or hypothesis must be stated clearly and in measurable terms. Note here that the reader can instantly see exactly what will count as observable evidence that the single-question children have performed better on conservation. They will have produced a count of more correct answers to a specific question. A poor wording of the research hypothesis would be:

> children do better in the single-question condition (an example of a poor hypothesis).

This does not tell the reader exactly how 'better' is assessed.

It is essential that you word your prediction or hypothesis in a precise manner (sometimes called 'operationalised'), otherwise your report will lose a specific number of marks (at A level and similar). This will be explicit in the marking criteria.

For qualitative studies with no specific hypothesis – see Frequently asked questions, page 115.

The method

This can be a rather dull section but, for markers, it is one where it is easy to knock off a good number of marks. The emphasis here is entirely on good detailed and complete description with special focus on detail. It is here that you tell the reader exactly what you did in enough depth for them to be able to go and repeat (replicate) it.

Most method sections divide up into four sub-headings and you would be advised always to use these in your report:

* **design**

- **participants**
- **materials/apparatus**
- **procedure.**

The section can be compared to the preparation of food from a recipe. The ingredients are your Participants. The tools you used are the Materials. The steps you took in preparing the food amounts to the Procedure. Finally, the overall type of food you made (cake, soup) is the Design. We won't push that analogy any further but just as with food, if you are not explicit and detailed enough, your reader won't be able to recreate what you did.

THE DESIGN

This is the *type* of method that you used. It is not the detailed steps that you took. Save these for the procedure. Here you can answer questions such as:

- **was it an experiment?**
- **if so, what kind? (repeated measures, independent samples, quasi-, naturalistic, etc.)**
- **what were the variables? (independent variable and its levels; dependent variable; other variables measured – e.g. for matching purposes) if there appears to be no independent variable or dependent variable then see FAQs, page 115**
- **were there different groups? (e.g. control, experimental, placebo)**
- **what controls were used? (counterbalancing, equivalent stimuli, random allocation, matching, etc.)**
- **if it was an observation study, what type? (participant, non-participant, structured, naturalistic, etc.)**
- **if it involved correlation which variables were compared with which others?**
- **was there a pilot study? (if so give purpose and design but no details).**

Don't feel you must select one only of the terms given as examples in brackets above. You might, for instance, be running a non-participant, structured and naturalistic observation study. The design simply sets out the main framework for the study so that the reader can see the logic of your overall method.

The easiest mistakes to make here are:

- too much detail which should be left for the procedure
- forgetting simple main aspects of the design (e.g. what kind of experiment?).

Projects in Practice

Design section for study on conservation

The research employed a matched pairs experimental design with one group given the standard two-question procedure and the other group receiving the experimental one-question procedure. Participants were matched on numeracy ability. The experiment was conducted in a field location (the children's classroom). Conservation ability was assessed as a correct answer ('the same') to a question asking whether two lumps of Playdo were the same or different after transformation.

Note here that we do not describe the questioning procedures in detail (leave that for the Procedure), nor do we give details of the children, the classroom or the exact question. This section serves a function rather like telling a cook following a recipe that we are going to use oven baking to make a cake, there are two stages and we will use some type of flour and butter combination.

For pilot studies – see Frequently asked questions, page 115.

THE PARTICIPANTS

The participants are a crucial aspect in your research design yet this section is often given short shrift in many practical reports. Recent critiques have shown that the vast majority of participants in psychological research are students in the USA or the UK. Therefore it is essential that you think carefully about who exactly you included in your study and give this precise information to your reader. You need to answer the following questions:

- how many participants altogether?
- how many in each group or condition?
- where were the participants from and how were they obtained? i.e. what was the *sampling method* employed?
- other features such as sex, geographical area, occupation (e.g. student), etc.

Don't claim that your sample was 'randomly selected'. It almost certainly wasn't because purely random samples are extremely rare in any psychological research (see page 32). What you may well have done is to randomly allocate all your available participants to the experimental conditions. Again you should say if and how this was achieved.

In the conservation experiment described earlier the children were matched on numeracy ability. This is a rare opportunity in student practicals but if it happened details should be supplied here.

MATERIALS/APPARATUS

You should describe accurately any equipment used, giving specifications of constructed equipment (finger-maze, illusion box) and source (manufacturer, make, model) of commercial items (software, projector). A description of all written materials should be given here though whole examples should be provided in an appendix. Examples are: word lists, questionnaires, scales, stimulus lists (pictures, objects) and so on. The rationale for selecting these particular sets of words or scales should be provided (e.g. a description of how two word lists were made equivalent). The nature of *some* materials can be taken for granted and not described – e.g. pencils, paper.

Do not list! What you should *not* do here is simply to provide a list of materials used. As with all other sections of your report, the information should be provided in prose text. That is, you should talk to your reader *about* what you used.

The source of questionnaires should be cited (and referenced later). If questionnaires have been developed from scratch during the project then there should be a description of how the measure was developed and any information, if possible, on its reliability or validity. A sample questionnaire should be included in the appendix section, unless it is a very well-known instrument.

PROCEDURE

This section is very similar to the way cooking instructions, mentioned earlier, are presented. The detail given here must enable a naïve reader to go through exactly the same steps as you did. The simplest thing to do is to 'walk through' the whole procedure as seen from one of your participants. If you start with 'Participants were ...' you shouldn't go far wrong in most cases. Take the reader through, in chronological order, what happened to the participants in both conditions. Use the following as an example.

Projects in Practice

Having agreed to run the study in class the headteacher and class teacher arranged to have parents sign a consent form permitting their child to be included in the research study. Only those with signed forms were included in the study.

On the day of testing, the researcher was introduced to the children as a friend who had come to 'play a few games about thinking'.

Participants were asked to sit at a table in a quiet room and were shown the experimental equipment (items and layout described above). In the control condition, when the child was paying attention, the researcher said:

'I have two balls of Playdo here. Which do you think has more Playdo or do you think they're both the same?' (A)

If the child answered 'the same' this was recorded and the procedure moved on to the next stage. If the child thought they were different the researcher asked:

'Which ball do you think has more?' (B)

The researcher removed a piece of Playdo from the ball perceived as larger then repeated the procedure until the child agreed that the two balls were equal.

In the second stage the researcher said 'Now watch very carefully', then rolled the left-hand ball into a sausage shape and then repeated question (A) above. The child's response was noted.

In the experimental condition the researcher said:

'I have two balls here and they have the same amount of Playdo in them.' The researcher then proceeded with the second stage just described.

Note that this procedure contains standardised instructions given in exactly the same form to every participant. This should reduce any variation caused by treating children differently. Of course there may be some variation outside the experimental procedure, for instance language used in order to encourage the child to concentrate in the first place. With adults, too, it is impossible to use exactly the same wording at all times since your participants will talk to you in different ways. However, the ideal is to use exactly the same wording for crucial stages of the data-gathering process, especially any task instructions.

It is also extremely important that you include here any ethical procedures such as debriefing. You can include in an appendix any consent forms you employed.

RESULTS

Description of results

It is important to see your results section as having two parts.

1 **A description in text of your results.**

2 **An 'analysis' of results, often a significance test, where appropriate.**

In this first descriptive section your text carries on the verbal style of the previous sections of the report. You tell your reader *in words* what you found. You can't just present a table of data. Tables and charts are *supplementary* aids to communication.

The statistics presented here are a *summary* only of the data you collected, presented as means, medians, standard deviations, frequencies, etc. Raw data (the participants' individual scores) should be presented in an appendix. Typically you will give your reader the descriptive statistics for each condition of an experiment, or for each group tested. Note that you are not required to present the mean, median *and* mode. You will be marked for *selecting* an appropriate summary statistic and only one type is required.

Treatment of results

Research in Practice 20 reports the analysis or 'treatment' of results. An inferential statistical test has been applied in order to test differences or correlations for significance. This is where you tell your reader *which* results you are going to test, exactly what test you are going to use, and *why* you are using that test. The 'why' consists of the answers to the three questions shown in Table 4, page 81, which initially helped you choose this test. To communicate the result clearly to your reader you need to include, preferably in this order, for each inferential test conducted:

1 **The obtained test statistic (e.g. 't = 2.14').**

2 **The degrees of freedom or the N (for both groups if an unrelated design).**

3　Whether a one- or two-tailed test is being conducted (and perhaps why).

4　The appropriate critical value (if using statistical tables).

5　The appropriate level of *p* (e.g. '*p* < 0.05' or '*NS*').

6　The final conclusion e.g. 'The difference between means is therefore significant and the hypothesis that caffeine improves Gameboy skills is supported'.

Research in Practice 20

Emma asked males and females to estimate their own IQ and that of their mother and their father. Her results ran as follows.

Results

As Table A shows, male participants did, as predicted, produce a higher estimated 'own IQ' mean of 110 (SD 14.14) than did female participants whose mean was 100 (SD 6.32). Also, both groups estimated a higher mean IQ for their fathers than for their mothers. The female standard deviations are generally lower than those for males and the standard deviation for fathers is lower overall than for mothers and 'own'.

Table A – Estimates of IQ for self, mother and father made by 6 male and female participants: mean (and standard deviation)

	Mean estimated IQ Own	Mother	Father
Participant sex			
Male	110 (14.14)	95 (14.14)	113 (10.30)
Female	100 (6.32)	97 (13.27)	109 (6.63)
Total	105 (11.67)	96 (13.11)	111 (8.52)

Treatment of results

Difference between male and female self-estimates

A Mann-Whitney test was applied to the differences between male and female estimated IQs since the design is unrelated and the data, being human estimates, are best

Continued

treated as ordinal for significance testing. This gave a U of 9.5 which gives $p > 0.05$ for a two-tailed test with $N_a = 6$ and $N_b = 6$. Therefore the difference between male and female self-estimates is not significant and Ho is retained.

Differences between estimated IQs for mothers and fathers

A Wilcoxon matched pairs, signed ranks test was applied to the differences between estimates of mothers' and fathers' IQs, since these are matched pairs (related data) and the scores are human estimates, treated as ordinal data for significance testing. This gave a T of 11 which gives $p < 0.05$, for a two-tailed test with $N = 12$. Therefore the difference between estimates for fathers and mothers may be taken as significant and HO is rejected.

Notes

- This results section contains a descriptive section (what happened) and an analysis or 'treatment' section (are differences or correlations significant?).

- The descriptive section is in text, supported by a table.

- The table is headed and it is obvious what the value of 110 (for 'male', 'own') is a measure of.

- The analysis section tells us: what test was used, on what results, what the test statistic was, whether the test was one-or two-tailed, N (or df), whether this difference is significant and at what level, and, finally, the overall conclusion of each test.

Dos and don'ts for the results section

- Don't just present a table entitled 'Results' and expect the reader to obtain from this all that you want to tell them about what happened.

- Don't call tables 'figures'; tables present data in tabular form; figures are charts or diagrams.

- Don't present too many statistics (e.g. mean, median and mode), just what is required for an appropriate summary.

- Don't present too many charts and tables so that the section is confusing. The reader only requires a clear, accessible summary of results.

- Don't just say 'the results'. For instance 'The results were analysed using a Spearman correlation', or 'The results show that males do worse than females'. *What* results?

- Don't just say 'the results were significant'. Which results? At what level? For what kind of test (e.g. one- or two-tailed; *df*?).

- Don't call the groups in your tables 'Group A' and 'Group B'. Give an informative label that tells the reader which groups these are.

- Don't copy material directly from computer programs.

- Don't report to large numbers of decimal places. Round up to your level of measurement accuracy. If scores were whole numbers then means should be to one place; if scores were to one place then means to two places and so on.

- Don't (following a computer program) report '$p = 0.000$'. This is impossible and the program only says this because it doesn't calculate to a greater number of decimal places. Use '$p < 0.01$' in this case.

- Don't show calculations in the results section. Put these in an appendix.

- Do start with a verbal description of results.

- Do head and label all charts and figures accurately. It should be easily possible to understand what units the numerical values are in (for instance 'inches' or 'number of words correctly recalled').

- Do state which results are to be analysed by a particular significance test.

- Do give your tables and charts an informative title. 'Results of the conservation test' is not a useful title.

- Do justify your selection of a significance test.

- Do report all details of the significance test: one- or two-tailed, critical value (where appropriate), *df* or *N*, level of probability (e.g. $p < 0.05$).

Discussion

Your discussion should do the following things.

1 Summarise your findings.

2 Relate these back to the predictions made in the introduction and the associated theory.

3 Evaluate your method.

4 Suggest modifications and extensions to the study based on the evaluation and the theoretical position.

Notes

- The summary of findings should do no more than highlight the main findings of the study, though it may draw attention also to any oddities in the data, such as a very high standard deviation for one group (that wasn't predicted) or the existence of one or two 'rogue' (very high or low) scores.

- These main findings should be related back to the original hypotheses and underlying theory. For the example in Research in Practice 20, we could say that the significant male/female estimation difference is support for the hypothesis that males estimate their intelligence to be higher than that of females which in turn might support a theory that judgements about the self are affected by popular stereotypes.

- Evaluation of method is necessary because you might *either have obtained a significant effect but for the wrong reasons, e.g. an uncontrolled confounding variable in your design, or* you might have found no effect because of such a variable. For instance, your participants may have performed as well in front of an audience as they did alone. They may well be inhibited by the audience but they may have also improved through practice, thus camouflaging the audience effect.

- Suggestions for changes should emerge from trying to counteract the weaknesses you have just highlighted. Don't use knee-jerk modifications such as 'we should have tested more participants'. Why, if you achieved a significant result? It 'worked' anyway. Don't claim 'We should have tested both sexes/ members of other cultures', etc. unless you can give a good reason for doing so.

- A modification following from the weakness just highlighted in the audience study would be to counterbalance conditions so that only half the participants experience the audience after the alone condition, while the other half experience the opposite order of conditions.

- Extensions to the study follow from the state of play established by *this* study. Again don't just add the possibility of testing other types of people unless you can justify this. An extension to the audience study might be to try *warning* people about the audience in order to reduce the audience effect, or suggesting to them that the audience are highly critical of students (where participants are students) in order to *increase* it.

In your discussion do not try to include new research and essay-type material, not prompted by the findings, which you want to 'show off' with, or for padding. If the work is generally relevant then it should have appeared in the Introduction section.

Most reports wind up with some form of 'final comment' or conclusion. This is not the Abstract over again but just an overall comment to wind up proceedings, possibly a summary comment on the overall findings, their relationship to the relevant model or theory and implications for the future.

References

There is just one main rule here:

> **If you referred to it directly somewhere in your text, include it. If you didn't refer to it, don't include it!**

If you wrote '... Gross (1992) argues that ...'. this is a reference. The date means you're telling the reader where you got the information from. If you happened to read Gross's textbook whilst preparing your practical or trying to write it up then Gross is *not* a reference. Strictly speaking, if you read about Hughes (1978) only in Gross, this is a *secondary reference.* You can say 'Hughes (1978) as cited in Gross (1996)' in your text, then give the Gross reference in the References section. In fact, secondary referencing is a matter of some current academic debate. What is essential is that the reader should be able to locate precisely the work you have referred to. This is the one and only purpose of referencing. Quotations should be referenced, with the page number. If you want to tell your reader what you read but didn't specifically refer to in your text, put these titles under the heading 'Bibliography'; this is not usually required.

Lay out your references in the way they appear at the back of this book. The following details are essential.

* **For a book: Author's name, initials, (year), *title*. Place of publication: publisher.**

* **For an article: Author's name, initials, (year), title. *Journal*, *vol.*, part, page numbers.**

Appendices

Appendices are like your actual appendix – not absolutely necessary and you could do without it. However, we include extra information here that would be distracting in the main text such as: instructions given to participants, memory list items, questionnaires, detailed scoring systems, calculations and so on. Your page numbering should continue onwards through these. Separate topics go in separate, numbered appendices ('Appendix 1', 'Appendix 2', etc.).

General presentation

Use page numbering throughout and don't forget that charts and tables, inserted later, also require a consecutive page number. A title page sets the whole project off well and a contents page helps the reader go to specific sections.

Frequently asked questions

DO I HAVE A PILOT STUDY AND, IF SO, WHERE DO I INCLUDE IT?

A pilot study is a kind of 'dress rehearsal' used to check out any unforeseen snags in your procedure or materials. Sometimes we conduct a pre-study in order to develop a scale of measurement. Another pre-study might involve having naïve colleagues rate pictures in order to see which are the more scary or more attractive ones for use in your main study. These are not pilot studies. A pilot study tries out the actual main design in order to look for problems.

If you used a pre-study to establish a measure or to decide on the strength of stimuli, or similar, then you can include a description of this procedure in your 'materials' section. If you did run a pilot study, then there are two common ways to report this. You can use a sub-heading just after your Method heading which says 'Pilot study', then go through the usual four sections of the pilot study as you would for the main one which will then follow. This is useful if the main study turned out to be quite different from the pilot study because of all the problems it uncovered. Alternatively, if the pilot threw up only a few snags, then you write the Method section in the normal way, describe the pilot study in the design section and then just mention, in each subsequent section, any alterations that were consequent upon the pilot study.

WHAT ABOUT QUALITATIVE STUDIES?

This text has not concentrated on the nature of qualitative studies in any great detail. Observations and studies of natural phenomena often gather qualitative data to start with and then these are quantified through some form of coding system, and very often some form of content analysis is then carried out – see page 70. If your course or syllabus permits purely qualitative studies – these are studies in which data are not altered to quantitative at any stage and where the analysis is of the non-numerical information that has been gathered – then you could try referring to one or more of the texts below or seeking further advice from your tutor.

Banister, P., Burman, E., Parker, I., Taylor, M. and Tindall, C. (1994) *Qualitative Methods in Psychology*. Buckingham: OUP.

Breakwell, G.M., Hammond, S. and Fife-Schaw, C. (1995) *Research Methods in Psychology*. London: Sage.

Bryman, A. and Burgess, R.G. (1994) *Analyzing Qualitative Data*. London: Routledge.

Coolican, H. (1999) *Research Methods and Statistics in Psychology* (third ed.). London: Hodder and Stoughton. Chapters 9 & 21.

Hayes, N.J. (1997) *Doing Qualitative Analysis in Psychology*. Hove: Psychology Press.

Mason, J. (1996) *Qualitative Researching*. London: Sage.

Richardson, J.T.E. (1996) *Handbook of Qualitative Research Methods for Psychology and the Social Sciences*. Leicester: British Psychological Society Books.

Robson, C. (1993) *Real World Research*. Oxford: Blackwell.

Smith, J.A., Harré, R. and Langenhove, L.V. (1995) *Rethinking Methods in Psychology*. London: Sage.

Strauss, A. and Corbin, J. (1990) *Basics of Qualitative Research*. London: Sage.

WHAT IF I DON'T HAVE AN INDEPENDENT VARIABLE OR DEPENDENT VARIABLE?

Many studies don't have an independent variable and a dependent variable. Strictly speaking, only true experiments have true independent variables. In a quasi-experiment, however, we would normally talk of an independent variable having an effect even though, in natural experiments, this is not manipulated by the experimenter. Remember that an independent variable is a variable which changes for different groups of participants but only, we hope, in one specific way (e.g. coffee or no coffee given to participants before a task). If we conduct a 'correlational' study – that is, we look for a relationship between two existing variables or we look for existing differences between two groups – then there is no independent variable being manipulated or even altered during the study. Hence, there is no independent variable. In the design section of such studies you need to define what each variable is and make clear what relationship is expected between them – e.g: 'a difference was expected on confidence scores between successful and unsuccessful sports persons'.

DOES IT MATTER IF MY PRACTICAL DIDN'T WORK?

No. The idea is to demonstrate the skills involved in designing, conducting and writing up research. You are not expected to be a successful research scientist with results ready to publish! There is often a lot more to say when things don't 'work' than when they do, making writing up rather easier. You will have plenty to say about the possible reasons for 'failure'. However, even if your study *does* produce a significant result, you must produce a critique of your design and method in the Discussion section.

AQA (Specification A) – specific requirements

Coursework issues

If you are following the AQA (A) course, there are a number of points you should consider before planning your coursework project:

1 **You are required to submit one piece of coursework.**

2 **This may be drawn from any content area of the A2 or AS specification.**

3 **The method used must be one of the following:**
   - **laboratory experiment**
   - **field experiment**
   - **natural experiment**
   - **survey**
   - **observational study**
   - **correlational research.**

4 **Data can be collected and analysed in groups of four people or fewer, but the write-up must be your individual work.**

5 **The results must be analysed using inferential statistics (statistical tests) such as:**
   - **chi-square**
   - **binomial sign test**
   - **Mann–Whitney U test**
   - **Wilcoxon matched pairs test**
   - **Spearman's rho**

   Other statistical tests (such as the t test and Pearson's product moment correlation) *may* be used although the use of these tests would need to be justified.

6 **You are required to complete a Project Brief (see Chapter 3) before starting any data collection.**

AQA (A) coursework assessment criteria

This section illustrates how the marks are awarded for your AQA (A) coursework project. A specific number of marks is allocated for specific parts or aspects of your coursework report. Knowing how these are allocated is important in trying to maximise the number of marks you can get for your report.

PROJECT BRIEF

The purpose of the project brief has already been mentioned in Chapter 3. You may remember that this is the part of your coursework where you include the sort of material that would not usually be found in a journal article (such as the advantages and disadvantages of the methods used, and identification of any ethical issues in your research). The marking criteria below, combined with the material in Chapter 3, will help you to construct an effective response to this aspect of your assessment.

Explanation of direction of hypothesis (1 mark)

For **1 mark** – you need to give an appropriate explanation of why a directional or non-directional hypothesis has been selected

For **0 marks** – there would be no explanation of why a directional or non-directional hypothesis has been selected or the explanation given would be inappropriate

Identification of research method/design (1 mark)

For **1 mark** – you must correctly identify the research method and research design you intend to use (if appropriate)

For **0 marks** – your research method and research design (if appropriate) would not have been identified or were wrongly identified

A B C D E F G H I J K L M N O P Q R S T U V W X Y Z

Identification of the advantages and disadvantages of the chosen research method (2 marks)

For **2 marks** – there should be a full explanation of the potential strengths and weaknesses of your chosen research method and/or design

For **1 mark** – there would be a partial explanation of the potential strengths and weaknesses of your chosen research method and/or design

For **0 marks** – there would be no explanation or an incorrect explanation of the potential strengths and weaknesses of your chosen research method and/or design

Identification of bias/confounding variables (2 marks)

For **2 marks** – you should identify any potential sources of bias and/or confounding variables

For **1 mark** – an attempt would be made to identify some relevant potential sources of bias and/or confounding variables

For **0 marks** – no relevant potential sources of bias and/or confounding variables would be identified or the sources of bias identified would be inappropriate or incorrect

Explanation of bias/confounding variables (2 marks)

For **2 marks** – you should give a full explanation of the procedures to be adopted to control the problems identified in the previous section

For **1 mark** – a partial explanation would be given of the procedures to be adopted to control the problems identified in the previous section

For **0 marks** – any procedures to be adopted to control the problems identified in the previous section would be ineffective or missing

Statistical significance (1 mark)

For **1 mark** – a suitable level of statistical significance should be selected

For **0 marks** – an unsuitable level of statistical significance would be selected

Identification of ethical considerations (3 marks)

For **3 marks** – you should fully identify any possible ethical considerations in your research and identify suitable steps to deal with these issues

For **2 marks** – some possible ethical considerations would be identified and suitable steps to deal with these issues would be identified

For **1 mark** – possible ethical considerations would be identified but the steps to deal with these issues are inadequate

For **0 marks** – possible ethical considerations would not be identified or they would be inappropriate or incorrect

THE REPORT

The report is your opportunity to produce an account of your work along the lines of a published study. Follow the different sections carefully as each of these is worth a certain number of marks. The report is not simply given a global mark at the end. The sections detailed below indicate the way you should structure your report and how the marks are won (or lost) in each of the different sections.

Implementation of the investigation

Some students will be given the opportunity to design their own research from scratch (see Chapter 1) whereas others will conduct studies that are completely designed by the teacher. You may not have to make this decision, but bear in mind the extra marks available for self-design or even what you might achieve as part of a small group (defined by AQA as up to four students). Whatever route you take, the write-up of your report must be entirely your own work.

Your contribution to the design of the investigation (3 marks)
Investigations can be designed by individual students, small groups or teachers

For **3 marks** – the design of the investigation must be entirely your own work. It might be an original design or an adaptation of a previously published work

For **2 marks** – the design of the investigation should be the work of a small group of students. It might be an original design or an adaptation of a previously published work

For **1 mark** – the investigation would be designed by you or a small group of students, but with support from a teacher

For **0 marks** – you will not have contributed to the design of the investigation

Marks are available for the competence that you show when designing your study, and the degree to which you consider, and correctly implement, important design decisions as suggested below.

Design decisions (3 marks)
These include choice of method, choice of experimental design, identification of variables, ethical considerations, etc.

For **3 marks** – given the aims of the investigation, design decisions have been applied appropriately and competently

For **2 marks** – design decisions have been applied appropriately with minor exceptions

For **1 mark** – design decisions have been applied weakly

For **0 marks** – design decisions have been applied inappropriately

Abstract

This is effectively a summary of the whole study. It should contain details of the main aims, methods, results and conclusions. AQA suggest that this section should be around 150 words.

Abstract (3 marks)
What was the study trying to do, what was done and to whom, what was found and what does it all mean?

For **3 marks** – your abstract must give clear and concise information on the main aims, methods, results and conclusions drawn from the investigation

For **2 marks** – your abstract should give information on either all or some of the points required for 3 marks, but it will lack an element of clarity or conciseness in its reporting style

For **1 mark** – your abstract will lack clarity or will draw attention to minimal information provided by the investigation

For **0 marks** – Either you do not provide an abstract or it is inappropriate

Introduction/Aims and hypotheses

This should not be a general essay, but it should move from background theory and research and end with the study's aims. It is your chance to demonstrate that you understand the basis of your study. AQA suggest that this section should be around 600 words.

For the aims you should explain the specific area of investigation and what you are trying to do. This represents your attempt to justify the hypotheses that follow and the direction of the hypothesis. For the hypotheses, you should state the experimental (alternative) hypothesis and the null hypothesis clearly and unambiguously.

Introduction: support from psychological literature (5 marks)
This should be concise and selective, starting with the general problem or underlying theory, moving through specific and relevant research studies and leading logically into the aims and hypotheses

For **5 marks** – you must support your investigation by relevant and carefully selected psychological literature

For **4 marks** – you may have supported your investigation by relevant and carefully selected psychological literature but there are omissions

For **3 marks** – you may have supported your investigation by relevant psychological literature but your choice of literature lacks selectivity

For **2 marks** – you may have supported your investigation by relevant psychological literature but there are important omissions

For **1 mark** – your investigation received minimal support from relevant psychological literature

For **0 marks** – your investigation received no support from relevant psychological literature

Aim(s)/Hypotheses: formulation (3 marks)
This should show a clear progression from the previous section and justify the direction of the hypotheses

For **3 marks** – your reporting must demonstrate a clear and logical progression from the background literature reviewed to a statement of the aims and/or hypotheses

For **2 marks** – your reporting should demonstrate, with minor exceptions, a logical progression from the background literature reviewed to a statement of the aims and/or hypotheses

For **1 mark** – your reporting will partially or inadequately demonstrate a logical progression from the background literature reviewed to a statement of the aims and/or hypotheses

For **0 marks** – your reporting will fail to demonstrate a logical progression from the background literature reviewed to a statement of the aims and/or hypotheses

Aim(s)/Hypotheses: statement (2 marks)
This should include a statement of the hypothesis and whether it is one- or two-tailed (directional or non-directional), and a statement of the minimum level of significance acceptable and why

For **2 marks** – your statement of the aims/hypotheses must demonstrate clarity and ease of testability

For **1 mark** – your statement of the aims/hypotheses may lack clarity or would be difficult to test precisely

For **0 marks** – your aims/hypotheses will be incorrect or missing

Method

A key criterion when assigning marks to this section is the degree to which your reporting of all the constituent parts of your study would allow accurate replication. Leaving out key details makes replication more difficult. Put yourself in the shoes of another student reading this section. What do you need to know to replicate the section exactly? Any stimulus materials, observation checklists, questionnaires and standardised instructions should not go in this section, but in an appendix. Also, you should watch your use of tense, as this is an account of what actually happened, not what you intend to happen. Therefore you should be writing in the past tense not the future tense. AQA suggest that this section should be around 600 words.

Reporting of method (4 marks)
This should include information about design decisions, participants, sampling, apparatus, procedure and controls

For **4 marks** – all aspects of the method used must be precisely and clearly reported in detail. Full replication would then be possible

For **3 marks** – reporting of the method should be described in sufficient detail for reasonable replication of the investigation to be possible

For **2 marks** – reporting of the method would lack detail, and replication of the investigation would be difficult

For **1 mark** – fundamental omissions in reporting the method mean that replication of the investigation would be very difficult

For **0 marks** – replication of the investigation would be impossible because of the lack of information

Results

This would include descriptive and graphical statistics, justification and details of inferential tests and significance. The first set of criteria applies to your selection (whether you pick the right techniques to summarise and analyse your results) and the second to the presentation of these techniques (see Chapter 16). Any raw data should not be included in this section but should be entered in an appendix.

Selection and application of techniques used for analysis (4 marks)

For **4 marks** – the selection and application of descriptive techniques and/or an inferential statistical test must be appropriate. The use of any inferential test must be justified with full reference to the data collected. An appropriate level of statistical significance must be applied and a full explanation of the actual level of significance reached provided

For **3 marks** – the selection and application of descriptive techniques and/or an inferential statistical test should be substantially appropriate. An appropriate attempt would be made to justify the use of the inferential test but without full reference to the data collected. An appropriate level of statistical significance would be applied

For **2 marks** – the selection and application of descriptive techniques and/or an inferential statistical test would be partially appropriate. A partially correct attempt would be made to justify the use of the inferential test and an appropriate level of statistical significance would be applied

For **1 mark** – you would take minimal opportunities to apply appropriate descriptive techniques and/or an inferential statistical test. The justification of the inferential statistical test would be incorrect and an inappropriate level of statistical significance applied

For **0 marks** – even though the use of descriptive techniques and/or an inferential statistical test would be appropriate, no attempt is made to use them. Alternatively inappropriate techniques were selected, appropriate techniques were applied incorrectly. Justification of the use of any inferential statistical test is absent

Presentation of data (4 marks)
Graphical or other descriptive statistics, inferential statistics (results of statistical tests), raw data in an appendix

For **4 marks** – descriptive and/or inferential statistics must be presented precisely and clearly. Presentation of raw data and calculations in an appendix must be clear

For **3 marks** – descriptive and/or inferential statistics should be presented in ways which, with only minor exceptions, are precise and clear. Presentation of raw data and calculations in an appendix should be clear with only minor exceptions

For **2 marks** – descriptive and/or inferential statistics would be presented in ways which showed some deficiencies in precision and/or clarity. Raw data and calculations are included in an appendix but their presentation lacks clarity

For **1 mark** – descriptive and/or inferential statistics would be presented in ways which show serious deficiencies in precision and/or clarity. Raw data and calculations are included in an appendix but there would be serious deficiencies in their presentation

For **0 marks** – even though they would be relevant, opportunities for presenting descriptive and/or inferential statistics are not employed. Alternatively, the attempts made are irrelevant or incorrect. Raw data and calculations are not included in the appendix.

Discussion

In this first part of the discussion you are required to explain how your findings match in with your aims and hypotheses. AQA suggest that the whole of the discussion section should be around 600 words, therefore this part should be around 150 words.

Explanation of findings (3 marks)
Includes relationship of findings to aims and hypotheses

For **3 marks** – the outcome of the investigation in terms of the hypothesis and/or aims must be explained in ways which are appropriate and coherent

For **2 marks** – the outcome of the investigation in terms of the hypothesis and/or aims should be explained in ways which, with only minor exceptions, are appropriate and coherent

For **1 mark** – an attempt would be made to explain the outcome of the investigation in terms of the hypothesis and/or aims although this would lack appropriateness and/or coherence

For **0 marks** – no attempt would be made to explain the outcome of the investigation in terms of the hypothesis and/or aims, or the attempt is irrelevant

The second set of marks is given for your discussion of how *your* findings relate to the research you described in the introduction section. It is also necessary for you to try and explain any inconsistencies between your findings and similar findings as reported in the introduction. As this section is also worth 3 marks, it should be approximately 150 words.

Relationship to background research (3 marks)
Includes a discussion of the findings with reference to the research used in the introduction section and an explanation of any inconsistencies

For **3 marks** – there must be a thorough discussion of the outcome of the investigation in terms of relevant background research

For **2 marks** – there should be a reasonably coherent discussion of the outcome of the investigation in terms of relevant background research

For **1 mark** – there would be limited discussion of the outcome of the investigation in terms of relevant background research

For **0 marks** – there would be no discussion of the outcome of the investigation in terms of relevant background research, or any attempt made to discuss the outcome would be irrelevant or incorrect

In this section marks are given for your ability to detect any limitations (e.g. problems with the sampling used or variables you should have controlled but didn't). You are also being assessed on your ability to overcome these problems (e.g. by suggesting a better form of sampling or describing how the problem variable might be better dealt with in the future). Again, this part of the discussion should be around 150 words.

Limitations and modifications (3 marks)
e.g. sampling flaws, lack of controls or ineffective statistical treatments and ways of overcoming these limitations

For **3 marks** – most limitations of the investigation should be reported, and appropriate modifications suggested

For **2 marks** – some limitations of the investigation should be reported, and some modifications suggested

For **1 mark** – there would be a partial awareness of limitations of the investigation, and/or occasional modifications suggested

For **0 marks** – limitations of the investigation would not be reported or would be reported inappropriately. Appropriate modifications would not be suggested

This often gives problems, but should be fairly straightforward. No research takes place in a vacuum, and so it is generally linked in some way either to a better understanding of some aspect of our behaviour or to an application of that understanding. Just ask yourself the simple question, 'So what?' What is the important lesson learned from this research? Also important is your ability to suggest where the research focus in this area might go from here. Were there some puzzling findings in the research, or some unanswered questions?

Implications and suggestions for further research (3 marks)
Includes ways in which the research might be extended and the wider implications of any findings

For **3 marks** – appropriate suggestions for further research must be mentioned, and implications of the findings discussed thoroughly

For **2 marks** – some appropriate suggestions for further research should be mentioned, and implications of the findings discussed reasonably coherently

For **1 mark** – an appropriate suggestion for further research should be mentioned, and there would be a limited discussion of the implications of the findings

For **0 marks** – suggestions for further research would not be mentioned or would be irrelevant, and implications of the findings would not be discussed

References

All key references should be included here, in the correct form and in alphabetical order.

References (2 marks) e.g. Cardwell, M. and Coolican, H. (2001).
A-Z Psychology Coursework Handbook. **London: Hodder & Stoughton**

For **2 marks** – all references must be provided in a conventional way for both sources used and studies quoted in the text

For **1 mark** – references would be provided in a conventional way but there are omissions

For **0 marks** – no references would be provided or the references included would not meet the normal conventions

Report style

Report style (3 marks)

For **3 marks** – your report must be concisely written in an appropriate scientific style (using a broad range of specialist terms), logically organised into sections and characterised by the adequate expression of ideas. There should be only minor errors in grammar, punctuation and spelling

For **2 marks** – the scientific style and logical structure of your report should be substantially evident with the use of a good range of specialist terms. There should be an adequate expression of adequate grammar, punctuation and spelling

For **1 mark** – your report would lack structure and would be written in a style inappropriate for a scientific report with the use of a limited range of specialist terms and a poor expression of ideas. There would be poor grammar, punctuation and spelling

For **0 marks** – it would be extremely difficult to tell if the report is based on a psychological investigation. The criteria for ideas, specialist terms, grammar, punctuation and spelling for 1 mark would not be met

AQA (Specification B) – specific requirements

AS level

The coursework component of the AQA (B) AS specification is fairly weighty, being worth 30 per cent of the total AS. Your practical investigation must be related to the content in either Module 1 ('Introducing Psychology') or Module 2 ('Social and Cognitive Psychology').

The sections detailed below indicate the way you should structure your report and how the marks are won (or lost) in each of the different sections.

DESIGN

One mark will be given for each of the following criteria (total 14 marks)

Aim stated

Background material

Hypothesis stated

Variables under investigation identified

Possible extraneous variable identified

Control suggested for extraneous variable

Target population identified

Sampling method identified

Sampling method justified

Task and materials described

Ethical issue identified

Control suggested for ethical issue

Procedure described

Procedure replicable

IMPLEMENTATION

One mark will be given for each of the following criteria (total 2 marks)

Evidence from reporting of appropriate treatment of participants

Evidence from reporting of procedures carried out appropriately

ANALYSIS AND INTERPRETATION

One mark will be given for each of the following criteria (total 10 marks)

Data represented in appropriate form(s)

Table(s)/chart(s)/graph(s) headed appropriately

Calculation(s) performed on raw data

Verbal summary of data

Results related to hypothesis

Results related to background material

Conclusion drawn

Appreciation of limitation of investigation

Suggestion for improvement of investigation

Suggestion for further research

COMMUNICATION

All components of report present (total 4 marks)

Use of terminology

Abstract presented

References presented

A2 level

Within the AQA (B) specification, coursework contributes an important role in the synoptic assessment of the course, so the following skills should be evident in your coursework. You should be able to demonstrate:

- **a critical understanding of possible experimental designs**
- **knowledge of how to use a specific research methodology**
- **your ability to evaluate scientific research**
- **an understanding of when to use appropriate statistical tests**
- **an appreciation of the strengths and weaknesses of quantitative and qualitative methods**
- **an understanding of issues related to the generalisation of research findings**
- **that you have considered ethical issues involved in research.**

Your investigation must be drawn from the content of the A2 specification (this is available on-line at www.aqa.org.uk) – that is A2 Modules 4 or 5. It must differ from the topic area of psychology that you chose for AS Module 3. Your coursework will be assessed in terms of four skills area as follows:

- **design**
- **implementation**
- **analysis and interpretation of data**
- **communication.**

The sections detailed below indicate the way you should structure your report and how the marks are won (or lost) in each of the different skill areas and different sections within those.

DESIGN

This assesses your ability to plan investigations – i.e. by using previous research and other background material, by formulating clear aims and hypotheses, and using appropriate methodologies. You should be able to:

- **identify and define a problem or testable hypothesis**
- **formulate a plan which could be used to carry out a practical experiment or investigation**
- **outline the procedure to be followed (identifying the variables to be investigated, the methods to be used to obtain information,**

ethical issues to be taken into account, any equipment/apparatus involved, etc.)

(AQA (B) Psychology specification document 2001–2)

Relevance of background material (4 marks)

For **4 marks** – background material chosen must be relevant to the investigation and commented on with appropriate critical appraisal

For **3 marks** – background material chosen should have relevance to the investigation and there would be limited critical appraisal of the material

For **2 marks** – background material chosen would be relevant to the investigation although there would be some important omissions

For **1 mark** – background material chosen would have limited relevance to the investigation

For **0 marks** –background material chosen would not be relevant

Formulation of aims (2 marks)

For **2 marks** – the reporting of the background material must demonstrate a logical progression for the formulation of an appropriate aim(s)

For **1 mark** – the reporting of the background material would partly demonstrate a logical progression for the formulation of an appropriate aim(s)

For **0 marks** – there would be no logical progression evident in the reporting of the background material and the formulation of the aim(s) would bear no relation to the material cited

Statement of hypotheses (2 marks)

For **2 marks** – the hypothesis(es) should be appropriately devised from the background material and should be testable/stated with clarity

For **1 mark** – the hypothesis(es) should have some relevance to the background material but lack clarity/testability

For **0 marks** – the hypothesis(es) would be inappropriate in relation to the background material or missing

Design decisions (4 marks)
Includes all essential elements (variables, controls, target population, sampling method, sample selected, procedures, task/materials and apparatus as appropriate)

For **4 marks** – detail of the method chosen must be justified and reported with clarity and brevity so that replication is possible

For **3 marks** – detail of the method chosen should have sufficient information so that reasonable replication is possible

For **2 marks** – detail of the method chosen would lack information so that replication would be difficult

For **1 mark** – serious omissions in the detail of the method would mean that replication is very difficult

For **0 marks** – it would not be possible to replicate the investigation from the information provided

Ethical considerations (4 marks)

For **4 marks** – all ethical issues relevant to the investigation should be reported in full and verbatim detail of contact with participants presented where appropriate

For **3 marks** –ethical issues relevant to the investigation should be reported and some detail of contact with participants presented

For **2 marks** – ethical issues would be considered although reporting would not be complete

For **1 mark** – ethical issues would be considered but not reported

For **0 marks** – there would be no consideration of ethical issues

A B C D E F G H I J K L M N O P Q R S T U V W X Y Z

Independence in design of the investigation (3 marks)

For **3 marks** – the design must be entirely your own work, either based on previous empirical research or on an original plan devised by you alone

For **2 marks** – you will have worked as a member of a small group to produce the design which is either based on previous empirical research or on an original plan

For **1 marks** – your design is supported by the teacher

For **0 marks** – you will have made no contribution to the design

IMPLEMENTATION

This refers to the collection of data, treatment of participants, use of materials/apparatus and procedures designed. You are expected to:

* **follow the procedure appropriate to the activity being used (including the use of any equipment) safely and with due regard to ethics**

* **deal with participants competently and with due regard to their welfare**

* **obtain information relevant to the investigation using the appropriate technique**

* **demonstrate independence in implementation of a design.**

(AQA (B) Psychology specification document 2001–2)

Implementation of design decisions (3 marks)

For **3 marks** – with reference to the design described, there should be clear evidence that decisions were carried out competently

For **2 marks** – with reference to the design described, decisions would have been carried out appropriately although there may be minor deficiencies

For **1 mark** – with reference to the design described, decisions would have been carried out poorly

For **0 marks** – implementation has failed to follow the design

Dealing with participants (3 marks)

For **3 marks** – clear evidence must be presented demonstrating appropriate interaction with and ethical treatment of participants

For **2 marks** – limited evidence would be presented with respect to competent interaction with and ethical treatment of participants

For **1 mark** – participants would have been dealt with competently although no evidence would be presented to support this

For **0 marks** – Participants would not have been dealt with competently

Independence in conduct of the investigation (2 marks)

For **2 marks** – you must have been entirely responsible for the conduct of the investigation

For **1 mark** – you would have been a member of a small group and you would have contributed to the conduct of the investigation

For **0 marks** – you would not have contributed to the conduct of the investigation

ANALYSIS AND INTERPRETATION OF DATA

You will be assessed on your treatment and analysis of data, the presentation of your data, your ability to relate your results to the aims and hypotheses and your evaluation of the investigation. You are, therefore, expected to:

- **choose an appropriate technique for analysis and interpretation of your data**

- **present data appropriately**

- **use information to reach conclusions, account for any variability, errors or limitations**

- **explain the outcomes and evaluate the effectiveness of the investigation according to its purpose, identifying as necessary any areas for improvement.**

(AQA (B) Psychology specification document 2001–2)

Choice and application of techniques for data analysis (4 marks)

For **4 marks** – qualitative, descriptive and inferential techniques would have been chosen and applied appropriately and with full justification. If relevant, significance levels would be appropriate

For **3 marks** – qualitative, descriptive and inferential techniques would have been chosen and applied mainly appropriately and with some justification. If relevant, significance levels would be appropriate

For **2 marks** – choices of techniques would be partially appropriate and justification limited

For **1 mark** – choices and justification would be barely discernible

For **0 marks** – no attempt would be made to choose and justify appropriate techniques or the attempts would be incorrect or irrelevant

Presentation of data (4 marks)

For **4 marks** – qualitative, descriptive and inferential data should be presented in appropriate summary form(s). Presentation should be clear and precise, and displays appropriately labelled

For **3 marks** – qualitative, descriptive and inferential data would be presented in appropriate summary form(s) with only minor deficiencies. Presentation would be largely clear and precise

For **2 marks** – qualitative, descriptive and inferential data would be presented with some deficiencies and presentation would lack clarity and precision

For **1 mark** – data presentation would be poor

For **0 marks** – no attempt would be made to present data or attempt is incorrect or irrelevant

Explanation of results (3 marks)

For **3 marks** – the results and analysis of the investigation must be explained in terms of the hypotheses and aims with clarity and coherence

For **2 marks** – the results and analysis of the investigation should be explained in terms of the hypotheses and aims with some clarity and coherence

For **1 mark** – explanation of the results of the investigation would lack clarity and coherence

For **0 marks** – no attempt would be made to explain the results of the investigation or the attempt would be incorrect or irrelevant

Relationship to background material (3 marks)

For **3 marks** – discussion of the results in relation to previously cited background material must be thorough

For **2 marks** – discussion of the results in relation to previously cited background material should be adequate

For **1 mark** – explanation of the results of the investigation would lack clarity and coherence

For **0 marks** – no attempt would be made to explain the results of the investigation or the attempt would be incorrect or irrelevant

Implications of results (2 marks)

For **2 marks** – implications of the results of the investigation must be discussed thoroughly

For **1 mark** – implications of the results of the investigation should be discussed

For **0 marks** – no attempt would be made to discuss the implications of the results or the attempt would be irrelevant

Limitations of generalisation (2 marks)

For **2 marks** – most limitations of the investigation should be discussed

For **1 mark** – some limitations of the investigation would be discussed

For **0 marks** – no attempt would be made to discuss the limitations of the results of the investigation or the attempt would be irrelevant

Suggestions for improvements (2 marks)

For **2 marks** – appropriate modifications to the investigation must be suggested

For **1 mark** – there would be a limited attempt to suggest modifications to the investigation

For **0 marks** – no attempt would be made to suggest modifications to the investigation or the suggestions would be irrelevant

Suggestions for further research (2 marks)

For **2 marks** – an appropriate suggestion for further research must be made and an explanation given for the suggestion

For **1 mark** – an appropriate suggestion for further research would be made

For **0 marks** – no suggestion for further research would be made

COMMUNICATION

In this final skill area, you will be assessed on the communication aspects of your investigation, using written, oral or other communication media. You are expected to:

* **present all components of your investigation using appropriate terminology**

* **adopt the required format for what is being reported as specified in the A2 specification**

* **be clear and precise in the presentation of information, especially that from other sources such as journals or published texts.**

(AQA (B) Psychology specification document 2001–2)

Written components (3 marks)

For **3 marks** – you must describe and present the report of the investigation with clarity, accuracy and in the required format

For **2 marks** – the report of your investigation should be described and presented with only minor deficiencies in clarity, accuracy and format

For **1 mark** – the report of your investigation would be described and presented adequately in terms of clarity, accuracy and format

For **0 marks** – the written components do not satisfy the threshold for 1 mark

Quality of communication (3 marks)

For **3 marks** – the report should be written with a high standard of literary expression. Spelling, punctuation and grammatical construction should be at a high standard, and specialist terminology appropriately employed

For **2 marks** – the report should be written with a good standard of literary expression. Spelling, punctuation and grammatical construction should be at a good standard, and some specialist terminology employed

For **1 mark** – the report would be written with an adequate standard of expression. Spelling, punctuation and grammatical construction would be adequate, but specialist terminology would be rarely employed

For **0 marks** – the threshold for 1 mark is not satisfied

Abstract (3 marks)

For **3 marks** – a brief and clear summary of the investigation must be presented which includes all relevant information

For **2 marks** – the summary presented would have some omissions or lack brevity

For **1 mark** – the summary would not be adequate

For **0 marks** – no summary would be provided

References (2 marks) e.g. **Cardwell, M. and Coolican, H. (2001).** *A–Z Psychology Coursework Handbook.* **London: Hodder & Stoughton**

For **2 marks** – all references should be presented in the conventional style

For **1 mark** – referencing would be incomplete

For **0 marks** – no references would be presented

Edexcel – specific requirements

AS

Coursework appears only in the AS component of the Edexcel Psychology specification. It is worth one third of the marks available for the AS. You are required to submit one coursework investigation of about 1500 words. You are expected to collect quantitative data in your coursework, and you could use either an experimental or a non-experimental method. Suitable methods include experiment, natural experiment, correlation, naturalistic observation, surveys/questionnaires and content analysis. Before embarking on your study, however, it is essential that you discuss it with your tutor in order to ensure that it is within the ethical guidelines laid down by the British Psychological Society (BPS). Edexcel publish a list of appropriate coursework suggestions. These are given below.

- **An experiment to see if interference affects recall in STM. In one condition participants rehearse and in the other an interference task blocks rehearsal.**

- **An observation of helping behaviour in a public place to look at gender differences (tallying is needed to guarantee that quantitative data is gathered).**

- **A questionnaire to look at age and sleep patterns.**

- **An experiment to see if a categorised list of words is recalled better than words not in categories when learnt. Variations of this idea are also acceptable.**

- **An experiment to see if deeper processing leads to better recall.**

- **A questionnaire to look at personality and attitudes (e.g. prejudice, but the questionnaire would have to be carefully worded and your teacher may prefer to submit it for approval).**

- **An experiment to see the effects of chunking on STM recall.**

- **An experiment to see the effect of imagery on recall.**

- An observation of behaviour in a crowded and non-crowded environment (you might choose a behaviour/body language and use tallying to produce quantitative behaviour).

- Interviews to look at everyday memory (categories would have to be developed to gather quantitative data).

- A questionnaire to look at the effects of seasons (daylight) or of shift work on bodily rhythms, e.g. sleep patterns or emotions or feeling tired.

(Edexcel Psychology Specification document, 2000)

Alternatively, you may choose another topic of your own design or an extension/replication of another study (see ideas elsewhere in this book). In this case, you will need to submit a brief outline of your intended study to Edexcel for approval.

Data for the investigation can be gathered by students *individually*, or in *small groups*, or within a *class* practical where each student acts as a participant, or within a class study where each student contributes, and where data are pooled (*Edexcel Psychology Specification document, 2000*). Data does not require the use of *inferential* statistics (statistical tests) but *descriptive* statistics should be used to analyse the results.

The aim of the coursework exercise is to give you the experience of gathering data and of writing up a report. You will need to be able to comment on the design of your study, and give alternatives, with reasons for their use. You will also need to be able to generate hypotheses, and to identify independent and dependent variables.

INTRODUCTION

This section should be concise and selective in its use of material, and should include the questions below.

- What theories and/or studies are relevant to this investigation?
- What study is being replicated (if any)?
- What is the aim(s) of the investigation?
- What are the hypotheses for the study?

Background research (10 marks)

For **8–10 marks** – relevant background theory/study must be concisely cited with increasing selectivity, accuracy or depth

For **6–7 marks** – background theory/study should be cited with increasing selectivity, accuracy or depth

For **3–5 marks** – there would be brief description of study/theory which is increasingly relevant to the study

For **0–2 marks** – background research would be missing or would be irrelevant to the study

Rationale (4 marks)

For **4 marks** – there must be a clear rationale for the study

For **3 marks** – there would be an increasing explanation of the link to the study

For **2 marks** – a clear link to the study would be made

For **1 mark** – a general link to the study would be made

For **0 marks** – no clear links would be described or would be missing

Aims (2 marks)

For **2 marks** – relevant aim(s) would be stated clearly

For **1 mark** – aim(s) would be stated but would lack clarity and relevance

For **0 marks** – aim(s) would be irrelevant or missing

Hypothesis(es) (2 marks)

For **2 marks** – the hypothesis(es) must be clear, concise and accurate

For **1 mark** – relevant hypothesis(es) should be stated

For **0 marks** – hypothesis(es) would be irrelevant to the study or missing

A B C D E F G H I J K L M N O P Q R S T U V W X Y Z

METHOD

Design and variables

* **What method is used (e.g. experiment, observation, correlation) and why has it been chosen as appropriate?**

* **What are the variables (e.g. IV and DV or related) in the study and how have they been operationalised?**

* **If an experiment is being conducted, what design has been chosen (e.g. independent measures, repeated measures or matched pairs) and why has this design been chosen as appropriate?**

Method and design (2 marks)

For **2 marks** – detailed and accurate method must be described, including appropriate justification for choice

For **1 mark** – the method would be described but an appropriate reason for its choice would be lacking

For **0 marks** – method used would be inappropriate or missing

Variables (2 marks)

For **2 marks** – variable(s) must be clearly identified and fully operationalised

For **1 mark** – variable(s) would be identified and operationalised

For **0 marks** – there would be no identification of variables

Participants

* **Who are the participants in the study with details (e.g. number, age range, sex ratio, etc.)?**

* **What is the target population and method of sampling (e.g. opportunity, random, self-selecting, etc.)?**

* **How are ethical considerations being dealt with in line with BPS guidelines on the use of participants?**

Participants (2 marks)

For **2 marks** – participant details and method of sampling must be clearly stated and justified

For **1 mark** – participant details and method of sampling would be stated

For **0 marks** – sampling technique and participant details would be inappropriate, unclear or missing

Apparatus

- **What equipment is involved in the study (e.g. word lists, scoring sheets, stopwatch, etc.)?**

- **What decisions are being made when designing the equipment (if appropriate)?**

Apparatus (2 marks)

For **2 marks** – suitable apparatus must be clearly described and choice justified

For **1 mark** – suitable apparatus should be described, including scoring system and origins if relevant

For **0 marks** – apparatus would be unsuitable or missing

Procedure

- **Where is each participant tested/observed etc. and under what conditions?**

- **How is each participant tested/observed etc.**

- **What are the standardised instructions given to each participant?**

- **How much time is allocated to each part of the study and for what reasons?**

- **Is the information given sufficient for the study to be fully replicable?**

Procedure (2 marks)

For **2 marks** – procedure must be clearly stated so that the study can easily be replicated

For **1 mark** – procedure would be stated and replication would be possible

For **0 marks** – procedure is unclear or missing. Replication would be difficult or impossible

Controls

* **What design, participant and situational variables (unwanted factors that could influence the results) are controlled for?**

Controls (2 marks)

For **2 marks** –awareness and possible control of extraneous variables or ethical considerations must be shown

For **1 mark** – awareness of extraneous variables or ethical considerations would be shown

For **0 marks** – identification of extraneous variables and control would be irrelevant or missing

RESULTS

In this section you should:

* **draw a summary table of results**
* **draw a table showing the measure of central tendency as appropriate for each condition of the study (e.g. mean, median, mode) and dispersion (e.g. range) as appropriate for each condition of the study**
* **draw an accurately labelled suitable graph (e.g. bar chart, histogram, pie chart, scattergraph, etc.) to illustrate the results for each condition if appropriate**
* **referring to the above table and graph(s), comment upon any trends found in the data for the conditions of the study**

- given the number of participants used, and the data obtained in each condition, explain which hypothesis (the experimental/alternate or the null) is most likely to be supported by the results of the study (allowing for a statistical test not having been carried out).

Summary table (2 marks)

For **2 marks** – an accurate, appropriate summary table using measures of central tendency or dispersion must be used

For **1 mark** – an attempt at a summary table or raw data would be made

For **0 marks** – a summary table of results would be inappropriate or missing

Summary table commentary (2 marks)

For **2 marks** – detailed, accurate and useful comments concerning trends shown in the table should be made

For **1 mark** – brief comments would be made describing the table

For **0 marks** – inappropriate or missing comments

Additional graphical description of results, e.g. graph, pie chart (2 marks)

For **2 marks** – an appropriately labelled clear description of results should be made

For **1 mark** – a suitable description of results would be made

For **0 marks** – an unsuitable choice of descriptive statistics would be made or they were missing

Descriptive results commentary (2 marks)

For **2 marks** – detailed, accurate and useful comments concerning any trends shown in the illustration should be made

For **1 mark** – brief comments describing the descriptive statistics would be made

For **0 marks** – inappropriate or missing comments

Relationship of results to hypothesis(es) (3 marks)

For **3 marks** – a detailed, clear and accurate explanation of how the results relate to the chosen hypothesis(es) should be given

For **2 marks** – an accurate explanation of the relationship between the results and the chosen hypothesis(es) would be given

For **1 mark** – an explanation of the relationship between the results and the chosen hypothesis(es) would be offered

For **0 marks** – inappropriate or missing explanation

DISCUSSION
Validity of the study

You should:

- **explain how valid the operationalisation of the variables was in the study (e.g. how well the test measured what it was supposed to measure)**

- **describe another, perhaps more valid, test that could have been used instead**

- **give a consideration of any problems with this new test, and explain why or why not there may be any problems with it.**

Validity (4 marks)

For **4 marks** – a fully informed concise discussion which assesses the validity of operationalisation of variables in the study should be offered

For **3 marks** – validity should be linked to operationalisation of variables

For **2 marks** – operationalisation of variables would be correctly identified

For **1 mark** – validity is referred to briefly

For **0 marks** – no reference to validity is made

Suggestions for improving validity (4 marks)

For **3–4 marks** – a detailed account should be offered of how more validity could be obtained, including the effects the suggestion might have on results

For **1–2 marks** – an increasingly detailed account of how more validity could be obtained would be offered

For **0 marks** – missing or inappropriate suggestions on how the study could be made more valid

Reliability of the study

You should cover the following topics.

* **Explain reasons why the study did, or did not, produce reliable results (e.g. if you did it again, would you get the same results?). Issues to consider include problems encountered whilst conducting the study, or issues concerning the methodology. These might include problems with the design, sampling, apparatus, testing conditions, standardised procedures, standardised instructions, and controls.**

* **Give a consideration of alternative methodological techniques (again looking at sampling, design, controls, procedure, etc.) that could have been used to conduct the study instead, and perhaps produce more reliable results.**

* **State whether there would be problems with these alternative methodological techniques, and explain why or why not.**

Reliability (4 marks)
Methodological issues including methodology, controls, sampling, apparatus, standardised procedure, standardised instructions

For **4 marks** – there should be a fully informed concise discussion which assesses the reliability of the study on a range of issues

For **3 marks** – reliability would be discussed with reference to more than one methodological issue

For **2 marks** – reliability would be referred to and linked to the study in one way

For **1 mark** – reliability of the study would be briefly referred to

For **0 marks** – no reference to reliability is made

Improving reliability (4 marks)

For **3–4 marks** – a suitable suggestion of an alternative technique should be made, including the effects the suggestion might have on results

For **1–2 marks** – increasingly suitable suggestion for an alternative technique would have been made

For **0 marks** – missing or inappropriate suggestions on how the study could be made more reliable

Implications of the study

You should:

- **explain what implications there are for the research outlined in the introduction to the study, and any limitations you have identified in the methodology**

- **explain what problems there might be in generalising the results to populations outside the target population**

- **give a consideration of at least one 'real-life' practical application of the results of the study.**

Implications of study (4 marks)

For **3–4 marks** – there should be a full and detailed discussion of the findings of the study in relation to the background research

For **1–2 marks** – an attempt has been made to relate the findings of the study with the background research

For **0 marks** – no awareness of the relationship between the results of the study and background research is evident

Generalisation of findings (2 marks)

For **2 marks** – generalisation of findings should be made to target population, and there should be an awareness of problems of generalisation to the outside target population

For **1 mark** – generalisation of findings would be made to the target population

For **0 marks** – no attempt to generalise findings to target population would be made

Application of study to everyday life (2 marks)

For **2 marks** – detailed description of how the study could be applied to everyday life should be made

For **1 mark** – brief links would have been made with everyday life situations

For **0 marks** – no application would have been offered

REFERENCES, APPENDICES, PRESENTATION OF REPORTS
References

Details of any references used should be recorded using the 'Harvard referencing system'. Book references are set out as in the example below. Journal articles may also be quoted, but you should include only those books and articles that you actually read/consulted. For example, if you read about Smith's 1998 research on neurotic behaviour in cats in McPherson's 2001 book on animal behaviour, you would quote: (Smith, 1998, cited in McPherson, 2001), and include the McPherson reference in your reference section (as this was the account you actually read).

Appendices

These should include:

- **raw data**
- **standardised instructions (if appropriate)**
- **stimulus materials**
- **any additional materials**
- **in the case of a questionnaire, a sample should be included, but it is not necessary to include all the completed questionnaires.**

References and appendices (3 marks) e.g. Cardwell, M. and Coolican, H. (2001). *A-Z Psychology Coursework Handbook.* **London: Hodder & Stoughton**

For **2–3 marks** – there would be an increasingly accurate list of references

For **0–1 mark** – references/appendices would be missing or incomplete

Presentation of report (2 marks)

For **2 marks** – appropriate format used; there should be good communication skills and a high standard of presentation

For **1 mark** correct format; communication skills and presentation would be increasingly clear, accurate and concise

For **0 marks** – correct format is not used. Poor use of communication skills, poor presentation

OCR – specific requirements

AS

For the coursework component of the OCR AS specification, you are required to carry out a practical activity in each of four specified areas. These will be kept in a 'Practical Investigations folder'. You will later be asked questions about these practical activities in your 'Psychological Investigations' examination paper.

These practical activities should be kept as simple and as short as possible. The aim is to raise issues and allow you to appreciate the difficulties of research, not for you to produce perfect pieces of work with complex designs and huge samples. Although texts (including this one) provide useful tips and ideas for practical investigations, most of these are too involved for AS level. It is more interesting and rewarding for you to develop your own ideas for this component of your course.

The four required practical areas are as follows:

1   Activity A: Questions, self-reports and questionnaires

Examples of appropriate activities in this area include:

- **a questionnaire on truthfulness**
- **self-assessment of mood**
- **a questionnaire on family relationships.**

2   Activity B: An observation

Examples of appropriate activities in this area include:

- **an observation of interactions between prisoners and warders**
- **an observation of the way adults hold babies**
- **an observation of mood.**

3 Activity C: Collection of data to investigate the difference between two conditions and an analysis using a Wilcoxon or Mann–Whitney test

Examples of appropriate activities in this area include:

* **an experiment to investigate the effect of the appearance of written work on the judgement of academic quality.**

4 Activity D: Collection of data involving two independent measures and analysis using a test of correlation

For **Activity A**, the following information should be recorded:

* **the aim of the investigation**
* **examples of the questions used, including any rating scales etc.**
* **details of the sample**
* **the procedure used to collect data**
* **a summary of results**
* **conclusions drawn from your findings.**

For **Activity B**, the following information should be recorded:

* **the aim of the investigation**
* **the categories of behaviour observed and the rating or coding system used**
* **details of the sample observed**
* **the procedure used for your observation**
* **a summary of your findings**
* **conclusions drawn from your findings.**

For **Activity C**, the following information should be recorded:

* **your alternative hypothesis and null hypothesis**
* **the variables used (i.e. IV, DV and any extraneous variables)**
* **the two conditions**
* **details of the sample used**
* **the design/procedure used**
* **the statistical test used to analyse the data**

- the results of your analysis
- conclusions, including statements of significance relating to your hypothesis
- presentation of data using tables, visual displays and verbal summaries
- computer print-out or manual calculations.

For **Activity D**, the following information should be recorded:

- your alternative hypothesis and null hypothesis
- the two variables used and how they were measured
- details of the sample used
- the procedure used
- presentation of data using tables, visual displays and verbal summaries
- the statistical test used to analyse the data
- the results of your analysis
- conclusions, including statements of significance relating to your hypothesis
- computer print-out or manual calculations.

As well as the information detailed above, it is wise to consider (although you should not record this in your folder) the following:

- ethical issues in your investigations
- the validity and reliability of the measurements
- alternative ways of measuring the variables
- the weaknesses in the methodology and ways of reducing them
- the advantages and disadvantages of each method/design.

Detailed examples of appropriate activities and how you might present these in your Practical Investigations folder are available in the *Teacher Support document for A level Psychology* (pp 15–28), available at www.ocr.org.uk. One word of caution, however, you must not copy the 'detailed examples' you find on this site, although you *are* allowed to use any of the 'further examples' given there.

A2

PRACTICAL REPORT

For this part of your coursework requirement with OCR, you are required to carry out and report on a piece of practical work that follows the traditional style of an empirical investigation in psychology. The report is written up in the standard report format and should contain a consideration of the following areas:

- **the theoretical context**
- **the chosen method**
- **the results of the investigation**
- **an evaluation of the investigation.**

The report for this component should be around 1200 words in length. OCR advise that practical activities should be kept as simple and as short as possible. Examples of appropriate research are available from the OCR website at www.ocr.org.uk.

The aim of the OCR project is to allow students to build on the skills they developed in the AS course and to design, conduct and report one complete piece of practical work. OCR reports gain marks by containing an appropriate theoretical content, making appropriate inferences about the material and about the data that is collected, and by using appropriate methods in a thoughtful and critical way. What is required is thoughtful and reflective work rather than rigorous research (*OCR Teacher Support document for A level Psychology*).

The sections below indicate the way you should structure your report and how the marks are won (or lost) in each of the different areas.

Abstract

This should be a summary of your general aims, method, sampling frame, results and conclusions. OCR advise that you should not write more than a paragraph for this section.

Abstract (2 marks)

For **2 marks** – there would be a fluent, clear description of the project and its findings

For **1 mark** – the overall aim, method and findings would be evident

Background/introduction

This section gives a rationale for the work that gives a theoretical justification and reasons for your choice of method. Points you might include are as follows (*OCR Psychology Specification document, 2000*):

- **background to the general area of study**
- **previous research**
- **terminology and concepts used in this area**
- **how the hypotheses for this study were developed**
- **reasons for your choice of method**
- **methodological considerations that may affect the results (for example, choice of sample)**
- **aims of the study.**

Background (3 marks)

For **3 marks** – the study is appropriately contextualised in psychological research and there is a clear rationale for the choice of method

For **1–2 marks** – a reasonable attempt would be made to describe and explain the psychological basis of the study and give reasons for the choice of method

Hypotheses or research aims

You should formally state the null and the experimental hypotheses in operational terms (i.e. define your concepts in the way that they are going to be measured). Alternatively, you state your research aims in a clear way that indicates how they will be achieved.

Hypotheses (2 marks)

For **2 marks** – there should be a clear operational hypothesis or research aim

For **1 mark** – there would be a reasonable attempt to frame an appropriate hypothesis or research aim

Method

This section should be divided up into the following sub-headings (*OCR Specification document, 2000*):

Design: type of study identified and described.

Participants: the population from which your sample was drawn (e.g. Year 13 psychology students), sampling framework, including number, type, age, allocation to conditions.

Procedure: how you developed the questions, how you approached the participants, standardised instructions and details of any materials you used. This section should be written so that someone reading it could repeat exactly what you did.

Controls: any controls you applied to the study, e.g. in the choice of participants, the behaviour of the experimenters, standardised instructions, and controlled time and place.

Measurement and analysis: how you chose to measure the variables, why you chose this measurement technique, the reliability of the measures, and how you have chosen to analyse the data.

Ethics: any ethical considerations that you had to consider and respond to.

Methodology (5 marks)
Points clearly expressed that are worthy of credit include appropriate details of: design, sample and sampling techniques, measurements of variable, details of procedure, controls and consideration of ethics. One mark for each to a maximum of 5

For **4–5 marks** – there would be a clear concise description of the methodology which would allow replication

For **1–3 marks** – a reasonable attempt would be made to describe the methodology of the study but there would be some omission of detail

Results

Many students nowadays have access to some very sophisticated IT and can present their data in equally sophisticated ways. The use of computer programs that analyse data and produce graphical representations of data are encouraged *provided* that the student puts the data into the program and works with the program to produce the output. Students must also identify the program they used, and show why they chose the particular form of analysis and presentation. (*OCR Teacher Support document for A level Psychology*)

Results should be presented as visually as possible, but you should also *describe* the data that you have obtained. It is very likely that you will use descriptive statistics of some sort (e.g. the average scores or the distribution of scores in the form of pie charts or block graphs/bar charts) and you should also consider whether it is appropriate to use inferential statistics.

Inferential statistics include statistical tests to evaluate the possibility that your results could have occurred by chance. You should give reasons for the choice of test and a significance level, significance statement. The workings for any statistical tests should appear in an appendix. (*OCR Psychology Specification document, 2000*)

Results (5 marks)
Aspects of the presentation of the results which when clearly expressed or displayed are worthy of 1 mark include: verbal summary, visual displays, descriptive statistics, inferential statistics, subjects' and investigators' reflections on the process, the meaning of the results

For **4–5 marks** – the appropriate use of summaries, tables and visual displays should clearly describe and demonstrate an understanding of the data, its analysis and conclusions

For **1–3 marks** – the data would be recorded in a comprehensible form. An attempt has been made to analyse the data and present the key aspects of the findings

Discussion

OCR advise the following format for this section (*OCR Psychology Specification document, 2000*):

1 **What do the results mean?**

2 **Can the null hypothesis be rejected?**

3 **What criticisms can be made of the method that was used? The method can be considered in terms of the following:**

   • **choice of design**

   • **choice of sample**

   • **choice of procedure**

   • **choice of location**

   • **choice of controls.**

4 **If the method had been changed in some way, how would this have affected the results?**

5 **Were there any confounding variables?**

6 **Were there any ethical issues raised during the study?**

7 **How do the results relate to the theory that was described in the introduction?**

8 **Do the results agree with or challenge the theory in any way?**

9 What modifications can be suggested to the theory in the light of this study?

10 Suggestions for further work.

Discussion (6 marks)
Aspects of the evaluation which when clearly expressed are worthy of 1 mark include: strengths of the measurement technique, weaknesses of the measurement technique, strengths of the methodology, weaknesses of the methodology, alternative methodologies, further research suggestions, usefulness or application of the results

For **4–6 marks** – most of the important methodological strengths and problems should be described and evaluated demonstrating understanding of the research process. Effective alterations to future studies should be suggested and the effects discussed

For **1–3 marks** – a reasonable attempt would be made to evaluate the effect of some of the methodological strengths and problems on the body. Some alterations with an indication of the likely effects or future studies would be suggested

---

References and appendices

Details of any references used should be recorded using the 'Harvard referencing system'. Book references are set out as in the example below. Journal articles may also be quoted, but you should include only those books and articles that you actually read/consulted. For example, if you read about Smith's 1998 research on neurotic behaviour in cats in McPherson's 2001 book on animal behaviour, you would quote: (Smith, 1998, cited in McPherson, 2001), and include the McPherson reference in your reference section (as this was the account you actually read).

Presentation, references and appendices (2 marks)
e.g. Cardwell, M. and Coolican, H. (2001). *A–Z Psychology*
***Coursework Handbook.* London: Hodder & Stoughton**

For **2 marks** – the report, its references and appendices should be presented clearly and concisely in the standard format

For **1 mark** – an attempt would be made to present the report, its references and appendices in the standard format

ASSIGNMENT

The assignment gives students the chance to demonstrate how psychology relates to a real life event. OCR recommend that this part of your coursework should be about 900 words (not including references). Marks are awarded for the accurate description of psychological knowledge, understanding (what the knowledge *means*), and application (applying psychological information to a new situation, and relating research findings to existing theories).

You will need to select, in discussion with your teacher, your own source for this assignment. It must be one that can be described and evaluated within a psychological context. After identifying the source of your assignment (i.e. the title (e.g. 'To diet for'), publication (*The Sunday Times*) and date (20 May, 2001), you should address the following three issues (*OCR Psychology Specification document, 2000*):

1   **What are the underlying psychological assumptions in or the issues raised by the source?**

2   **Describe and relate some psychological evidence to the source.**

3   **How can psychological evidence be used to affect the issues raised by the source?**

Assumptions or issues (5 marks)

For **4–5 marks** – assumptions or issues should be clearly identified and related to appropriate psychology. This should be clearly expressed and fluently written

For **1–3 marks** – an attempt would be made to identify assumptions or issues and relate them to psychology

Results (9 marks)
For the best three pieces of evidence, 3 marks for each piece of evidence

For **3 marks** – you must describe the evidence and relate it to the source in a way that demonstrates understanding and the relevance of the evidence to the source. This should be clearly expressed and fluently written

For **1–2 marks** – an attempt would be made to describe and relate psychological evidence to the source

Application (6 marks)
For the best three suggestions, 2 marks each

For **2 marks** – your suggestion must apply psychological knowledge demonstrating an understanding of and a pragmatic (i.e. logical) approach to the assumptions and issues raised by the source

For **1 mark** – the suggestion would attempt to apply psychological knowledge to the assumptions or issues raised by the source

Terms and concepts (3 marks)
Throughout the whole assignment

For **3 marks** – you should use a range of psychological terms and concepts appropriately and with understanding

For **1–2 marks** – some psychological terms and concepts would be used

Presentation, style and references (2 marks)

For **2 marks** – your presentation, grammar, spelling, punctuation and references would be good

For **1 mark** – your presentation, grammar, spelling, punctuation and references would be adequate although there would be some errors or omissions

A B C D E F G H I J K L M N O P Q R S T U V W X Y Z

Using information and communications technology in your coursework

You will already have come across information and communications technology (ICT) in your school experience. This may have taken the form of using specific software in class (e.g. maths packages) or more sophisticated uses such as word-processing and spreadsheets. The aim of this chapter is not to teach you these skills, but to show how they might be harnessed to improve the overall quality of your coursework. ICT refers to the applications (such as word-processing and graphics) and software (specially written programs that carry out these applications) that can be used to make your coursework investigation a little more professional. This doesn't just mean that it can be made to look more professional, but the conduct of the study itself can be improved by taking advantage of the various ICT opportunities open to you.

How can I introduce ICT into my coursework?

The major ICT applications which may be useful in your coursework are as follows:

- **word-processing packages (such as Word 2000)**
- **spreadsheets (such as Microsoft Excel)**
- **graphics packages**
- **the internet**
- **e-mail**
- **databases**
- **CD-ROMS.**

ICT can be introduced into your coursework through any of the above applications, but you are most likely to use these to:

- **gather information or data for your study (e.g. doing a literature search for appropriate information to provide a context for your study)**

- collect information and manage the progress of the study

- analyse the data using statistical packages

- word-process your report and present your data in tables and charts.

Gathering information using ICT

CD-ROMS

If you are lucky, you may have access to PsychINFO, a CD-ROM-based collection of abstracts of research studies in just the area you are looking for. Most universities and some colleges subscribe either to PsychINFO or to equivalent searchable databases such as E-Psyche. You may find that your local university library allows non-university students access to these resources, but ask first, and you may just be granted permission to use these resources on-site.

THE INTERNET

Search engines

These are computer programs that will locate websites based on whatever criterion you have entered in the 'search' location. Three of the most useful for searching psychology sites are: Altavista (www.altavista.com), Yahoo (www.yahoo.com) and Google (www.google.com).

1 **Altavista**

   Entering the Altavista address will bring you to the home page, containing the 'Altavista Directory'. From the category 'Library and Resources', go to 'Society', choose 'Social Science' and then 'Psychology'. Click on this and you will be taken to the subcategories of psychology (see screen shot below). Clicking on any of these will take you to sites of interest in that field of psychology.

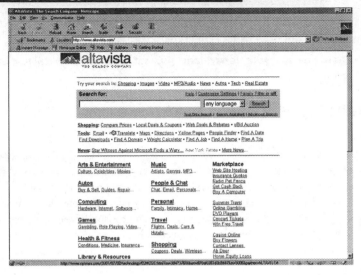

2 Yahoo

This is another search engine that provides links to different categories of psychology. From the home page (www.yahoo.com) click on 'Social Science', then 'Branches' on the next page. The numbers in brackets tell you how many sites are available for each category. Be patient, some of these will be no use at all to you, but every so often you will come across a real gem of a site. Bookmark it and you will be able to come back to it later.

3 Google

This may well become the one you use almost all the time, being the search engine of choice for most students and academics. It is quick and selective, so clicking on 'other sites like this' will take you to sites of a similar *level* (e.g. other university sites) elsewhere on the web.

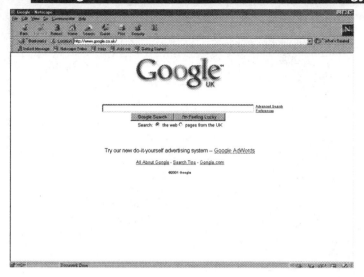

Meta-sites

There are an increasing number of sites on the internet that gather together information about psychology sites in one place. Two of the most impressive of these are Psych Web (www.psychwww.com) and Psych Site (http://stange.simplenet.com/psycsite). Psych Web in particular brings together a staggering number of psychology sites, and groups them into categories for you (see 'Scholarly Resources in order by topic').

If you simply want a bit more information about a topic, try www.about.com, and like the search engines above, it will take you to somewhere you can find it. If you get really keen, and would like to read some of the most significant full text works in the history of psychology, then Classics in the History of Psychology (www.yorku.ca/dept/psych/classics) is just the site you need. Why bother reading other people's accounts of famous research when you can read it yourself. That's what real psychology is all about.

A
B
C
D
E
F
G
H
I
J
K
L
M
N
O
P
Q
R
S
T
U
V
W
X
Y
Z

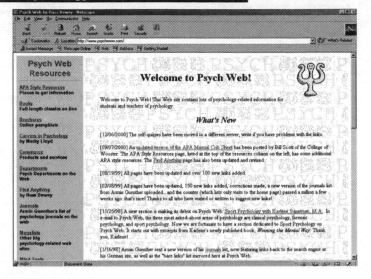

Presentation skills

This section is based around Microsoft Word 2000, although other word-processing packages will operate in much the same way, and produce much the same results. There are plenty of easy-to-follow guidebooks for every conceivable word-processing package that will enhance your presentation if you follow some fairly easy steps. Remember though, it is the quality of the material that counts, not the number of different fonts and pie charts you can muster to give the appearance that what you are writing is better than it actually is. Go for quiet clarity when presenting a report rather than outrageous flash.

MICROSOFT WORD

The Word window

Word provides a range of different 'toolbars' which sit at the top of your screen and enable you to carry out commands easily and quickly. Don't clutter your screen up. The most useful information that you will probably want open at all times will be available from four 'bars' at the top of your screen. These are as follows:

- **the title bar – this tells you the name of the file you are working on**

- the **menu bar** – this contains the main menus which give you access to various commands connected with the file you are working on, tables, help, etc.

- the **standard toolbar** – this contains 'buttons' for your most frequently used commands (such as 'save', 'print', 'undo'). You can customise this to include only the commands you want to be there

- the **formatting toolbar** – this gives you instant access to the various layout options that you will use in your report (such as 'bold', 'underline', 'bullet points' and 'change font size').

Practise using the various buttons to see what they do. How, for example, do you check your spelling and grammar? (The ABC button on the **formatting toolbar** is a handy one to use regularly as you are marked on your 'Quality of Written Communication' (*QWoC*) throughout your coursework reports.)

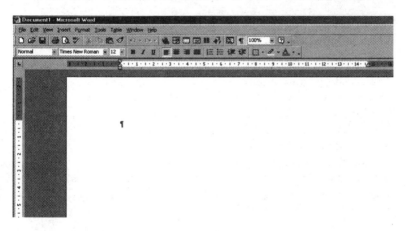

Creating tables

If you are using Microsoft Word, creating a table is extremely straightforward.

1   Click on **Table** in the menu bar. Choose the **Insert** option, then **Table** from the submenu that pops up. (See screenshot overleaf.)

2   When the **Insert Table** dialogue box opens, you can choose how many columns and rows you want in your table. Don't worry if you over- or under-estimate at this point, you can always add or delete rows and columns later. Click on **OK** to confirm your choice.

3   Add your data, remembering to leave space for column headings. The entries in the table can then be played around with to increase their 'readability'. In the table below, the participant numbers have been emboldened using the **formatting toolbar** command for bold (**B**). The data in the three conditions columns have been centralised using the **Centred Text** command also found on the **Formatting toolbar**.

4   If you need to re-size your columns because an entry is too big for the column available, simply place the insertion point (using your mouse) over the column divider to be re-sized, hold down the left mouse button, and the point will change to double vertical lines with inward facing arrows. Keeping the mouse button depressed, simply drag the column divider until you have the right size column.

5 There are lots of wonderful formats available for your table. To jazz up your table, click anywhere in the table to be formatted. Click on **Table** in the menu bar and then choose **Table AutoFormat** in the menu that pops up.

From this you can choose all kinds of formatting for your table. Try to keep it relatively simple, the information in tables can sometimes be difficult to understand if bright colours and visual effects have been over-used. The rather fetching **3D Effects 3** has been chosen to make our table that little bit more professional without being too brash.

A B C D E F G H I J K L M N O P Q R S T U V W X Y Z

6   Finally, no table is complete, you might think, without a nice border
    around it. Click on View in your menu bar, and then Toolbars from the
    menu that pops up. Click on Tables and Borders from the choice
    available, and an extra toolbar will appear at the top of your screen.

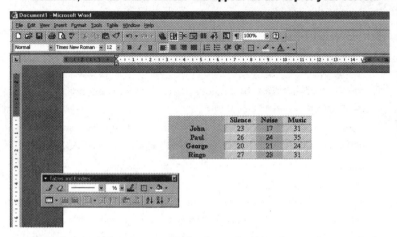

You can now choose your border from the drop-down menu, and after
clicking on the pencil icon, apply it to your table as if you were drawing
it with the pencil. Don't worry if you make a mistake, there's a rubber
available on the same toolbar! Again going for quiet understatement,
we have opted for a simple double line as a border.

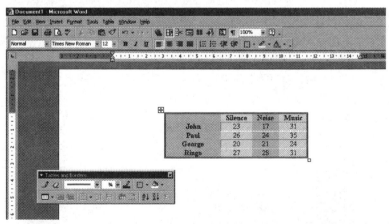

There are many more exciting things you can do with your tables,
but you have to know when to stop (there are other things in life

after all), so we'll stop here. Do remember that all tables should be properly titled, and should contain enough information be read and understood by anyone interested enough to look at them.

Creating graphs

You can either create a graph using an existing table, or create one from scratch. First, let's convert our table into a simple bar chart.

1   Highlight your table and copy it (**Ctrl and S** on your keyboard). Paste this copy of your table to the spot where you want your chart to appear (**Ctrl and V** on your keyboard).

2   Now highlight the whole table by holding down the left mouse button and dragging the curser across the table until it is all highlighted.

3   Click on the **Insert** command in your menu bar, and choose **Object**.

4   When this dialogue box opens, scroll down the different options and click on **Microsoft Graph 2000 Chart** (or **Microsoft Graph 97 Chart** if you have an earlier version).

5   Now you have a data sheet, the table and a bar chart as below. Things look a little crowded, but you can change that easily enough. Remove the datasheet by clicking on the **X** in the top right of the sheet, and remove the table by highlighting it, clicking on **Table** in your menu bar, and selecting **Delete** then **Table**. Both of these will now disappear and the chart will mysteriously jump into the space they occupied! You can play around with the chart by moving it around, making it bigger or smaller until you're satisfied with the way that it looks.

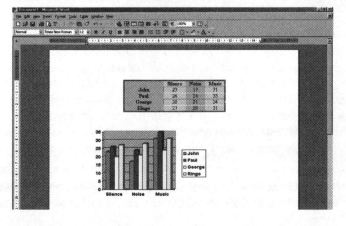

As with the table earlier, the chart should be properly titled and labelled. In order to add these, double click on your chart, select **Chart** from the menu bar that appears at the top of the screen, then **Chart Options** from the submenu that appears from there. Play around with this and you will soon learn what works and what simply doesn't look right. The example below shows one option:

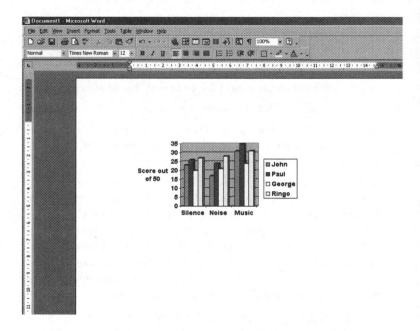

If you want to create a chart from scratch, place the cursor where you want the chart to appear in your document, and as before, click on the **Insert** command in your menu bar, and choose **Object**. When this dialogue box opens, scroll down the different options and click on **Microsoft Graph 2000 Chart**. A datasheet and a bar chart appear with some strange sample data. Click on the first column and type in your own column heading, and so on throughout the table, deleting or adding columns and rows as required. You can then follow the steps as before to label and title this chart.

You can change the chart type by double clicking on the chart, and from the **Chart** menu at the top of the screen, choose **Chart Types.** Select whichever chart you require and off you go again.

Ultimately you will need to experiment with charts and tables, and a specialist book that deals with this (such as the Dorling Kindersley *Tables, Charts and Graphs* by Sue Etherington) will save you a lot of time. As with all aspects of ICT, it can help make your work a lot easier, but it can also cause you many frustrations along the way.

Research suggestions

INTRODUCTION

Although all of the exam boards give credit for research you have designed yourself, getting the first idea and turning it into an actual research project can be quite intimidating. The five studies in this chapter are intended to give you a few ideas about what you might study, and how you might carry out a decent investigation in that area.

Subject to any penalties composed by your specification for the lack of *original* work (see Chapters 12–15), you may choose to simply carry out the study as suggested here. Alternatively, you could use these studies as a springboard to develop your own hypotheses (and therefore your own study) within a particular area.

The following studies have been chosen because they offer an opportunity to study real-life behaviour away from the confines of a laboratory. Do remember that some of these studies (most notably the study of ageing and cognition, and the gender differences in aggression among schoolchildren) pose important ethical questions for you. Make sure you discuss the execution of these studies with your teacher *before* you attempt to collect any data.

Mate choice and the lonely hearts columns

Darwinians view attractiveness in terms of reproductive fitness. Features that are positive indicators of reproductive fitness in a potential mate should be viewed as attractive by males and females. It is also clear that in most relationships men and women make an appreciable investment of time and energy. Consequently, both sexes should be selective about future partners, but in different ways (Cartwright, 2000). Of all the features used in appraising a potential mate, two in particular reveal inherent differences between male and female taste. They are physical attractiveness in females and the status of males. In the case of male status, the application of evolutionary principles predict that, since females make a heavy investment in raising young and since bi-parental care is needed following birth, females will be attracted to males who show signs of being able to bring resources to the relationship. If females respond to indicators of potential provisioning and status then males should be attracted to females who appear fecund and physically capable of caring for children. Since the period of female fertility (roughly the ages of 13–45) occupies a narrower age band than that of the male (roughly the ages of 13–65) we would also expect the age of prospective partners to be evaluated differently by each sex. Men should be fussier about age than women and hence rate physical features that correlate with youth and fertility higher on a scale of importance than women.

An intriguing way to gather information on mating preferences is to inspect the content of 'lonely hearts' advertisements in the personal columns of newspapers and magazines. A typical advertisement is shown below:

```
Professional male, 49, graduate, homeowner, good
sense of humour, seeks younger slim woman for
friendship and romance.
```

Notice that the advertisement offers information about the advertiser as well as his preferences for a mate. Such information carries some advantages over questionnaire response surveys in that it is less intrusive and less subject to the well-known phenomenon of interviewees tending to comply with what they take to be the expectations of the questioner (Cartwright, 2000). Moreover, the data is 'serious' in that it represents the attempts of real people to secure real partners.

This study investigates whether the predictions that might arise from Darwinian evolutionary theory are reflected in the way in which males and females advertise for mates. By utilising the 'lonely hearts' columns, it enables us to gather real-life data in a relatively unobstrusive manner. Remember that the important thing in these advertisements is not whether people are telling the truth about themselves, but that they are expressing what is important to them (when advertising for a mate) and what they feel is important to others (when advertising *themselves* as a mate).

> 'This is the point at which people demand the most from a potential mate and claim to be offering the most themselves. Eventually, the bids might be lowered, but this first stage provides a glimpse into what men and women consider the ideals.'
>
> *(Dunbar, 1995)*

Waynforth and Dunbar (1995) analysed 479 newspaper advertisements placed by males and 402 placed by females. When it came to age, Waynforth and Dunbar's predictions proved accurate, with men generally preferring women between 1 and 12 years younger than them, and women preferring men between 2 and 7 years older. When it came to financial resources and physical attractiveness, the researchers' predictions were similarly borne out. Men, on average, boasted of their material wealth 1.7 times more often than women, while women demanded wealth 4.5 times more often, with the greatest number of demands being made when the women were between the ages of 20 and 39 – their peak reproductive years. Similarly, males offered cues to their physical attractiveness 1.4 times less frequently than females and demanded physical attractiveness twice as often. The greatest number of men expressed such preferences between the ages of 40 and 49 – a time when their earning power would be expected to be at its peak.

PREDICTIONS

There is a range of possible predictions arising from evolutionary psychology that can be tested from data provided in the 'lonely hearts' columns. These include those listed below.

Wealth/status

* Females ask for financial resources and economic security more than males.

* Males offer financial resources more than do females.

Physical attractiveness

* Males ask for characteristics indicating physical attractiveness more than do females.

* Females offer characteristics indicating physical attractiveness more than do males.

Age

* Females ask for males who are older than they are.

* Males ask for females who are younger than they are.

Family commitment

* Females ask for family commitment more than do males.

* Males offer family commitment more than do females.

METHOD

You should get hold of a range of publications that contain personal advertisements of people seeking partners ('lonely hearts' columns). These are more likely to be found in local newspapers (e.g. the *Liverpool Echo* or the *Bristol Evening Post)* and trade papers (such as *Trade It* that contain purely advertisements). You can then collect examples of male and female advertisers looking for partners. Do not be overly selective at this point (i.e. looking only for examples that confirm your hypotheses) as this will bias your results. Look through each advertisement for information relevant to your chosen prediction(s), and record the frequency with which these characteristics are mentioned. For each advertisement, you may find it useful to record the following:

1 advertiser's sex

2 advertiser's age

3 number of terms relating to physical attractiveness offered

4 number of terms relating to physical attractiveness asked for

5 number of terms relating to wealth/status offered

6 number of terms relating to wealth/status asked for

7 number of terms relating to family commitment offered

8 number of terms relating to family commitment asked for

9 lowest age in the range requested for potential partner

10 highest age in the range requested for potential partner

11 sex of person sought.

Terms indicating physical attractiveness

The advertiser claims to be good-looking or seeks a good-looking partner. Terms such as 'beautiful', 'cute', 'fit', 'medium build', 'cuddly', 'nice-looking', 'sexy'.

Males may also use terms such as 'handsome', 'muscular', 'rugged' or 'tall'. Females may describe themselves as 'curvy', 'feminine', 'shapely', 'slim' *or* 'full-figured'. Some adverts will also allude to characteristics considered attractive in that sex (e.g. 'Sean Connery look-a-like; 40 years old but with the body of a 20 year old').

Terms indicating wealth and status

Any terms indicating home-ownership, professional status, education, or simply 'well-off'. These include 'affluent', 'well-educated', 'graduate', 'intelligent', 'enjoys the good things in life', 'company director', 'sugar daddy', 'industrious', 'solvent', 'successful' or 'well-to-do'.

Terms indicating age

Ages are sometimes indicated directly, but may be implied rather than stated, e.g. 'young at heart', 'youthful', 'active', 'healthy' or 'great shape for age'.

Terms indicating family commitment

Advertisers may suggest a willingness to participate in family affairs, e.g. 'caring', 'dependable', 'generous', 'family-minded', 'good cook', 'likes/wants children'.

ANALYSING THE DATA

The difference between males and females in respect to the chosen hypotheses can be represented in data summary tables and in bar charts. In order to see if any observed differences are statistically significant, data can also be analysed using the chi-square test of association (see Chapter 10). This statistical test requires independent data, meaning that each advertiser can only contribute to one of the categories being analysed. This means that if one of your 'advertisers' (i.e. a male or female) both offers financial resources and also asks for financial resources, they should not be used on this table. An example of the data that might be subjected to this analysis is as follows:

Table 19 Number of male and female advertisers offering or asking for financial resources

	Offering financial resources	Asking for financial resources
Males	37	6
Females	7	22

DISCUSSION POINTS

The results of this study can be compared to the findings of Waynforth and Dunbar, and to the predictions from evolutionary psychology suggested by writers such as Buss (1994). You should consider the implications of this study – is this compelling evidence that human mate choice is influenced by sexual selection? You might also comment on any other insights from your analysis of 'lonely hearts' columns. Dunbar, for example, noticed that men put their height in their advertisements only if they were tall. He suggested that people only advertise things that are advantageous. There may be several reasons why women prefer tall men. Society generally associates tall men with wealth, success and good health. Dunbar claimed that because the effect is so prominent, this preference may be programmed into women's genes. This could date back to a time when tall men in hunting societies were stronger and genetically better equipped for the struggle to survive. You might also consider whether the mate preferences studied here are evident in all cultures. Buss (1989) suggests that they are, but with some interesting discrepancies to this argument.

REFERENCES

Buss, D. (1989). 'Sex differences in human mate preferences'. *Behavioural & Brain Sciences*. Vol. 12, 1–49.

Buss, D. (1994). *The Evolution of Desire*. New York: Basic Books.

Dunbar, R. (1995). 'Are you lonesome tonight?'. *New Scientist*, Vol. 145, No. 1964, p.26.

Waynforth, D. and Dunbar, R. (1995). 'Conditional mate choice strategies in humans: Evidence from 'lonely hearts' advertisements'. *Behaviour*, 132: 755–779.

Social loafing: An investigation of collaboration effects in the music of Lennon and McCartney

INTRODUCTION

The term 'social loafing' refers to the tendency for people to expend less effort on a task in groups than they do when alone. Social loafing is most evident in additive tasks, i.e. those tasks where the contributions of each group member is combined into a group product. In such situations it becomes difficult to identify the contributions of any one individual, so people socially 'loaf'. Simply believing that others are likely to loaf means that we are likely to loaf also. According to equity theory we aim to receive out of a situation something roughly equivalent to what we put in. If we feel that others are not working as hard as we are we will then adjust our own output to match theirs.

Early investigations of social loafing were exclusively concerned with the quantity of effort produced by members in a group. In 1982, however, Jackson and Padgett extended the previously laboratory-based research to creative and artistic endeavours. These researchers were interested in the effects of group size on the composition of pop songs, proposing that 'if social loafing occurs in artistic creation as it does in other group situations, jointly conceived creations should reflect less effort than individually created works'.

In order to assess this proposal, Jackson and Padgett examined the creative output of the songwriting talents of Paul McCartney and John Lennon of the Beatles. Although most of the Beatles' catalogue is credited to Lennon and McCartney, only a small proportion of the songs composed were actually the result of collaboration. Drawing on the motivational losses explanation for social loafing, Jackson and Padgett (1982) suggested that a precondition for observing social loafing would be identifiability for solo-authored and relative anonymity for collaboratively authored songs. Biographers of the Beatles have identified two distinct phases in the group's career in which it is likely that their feelings of 'identifiability' changed. In the first, lasting until around the end of 1966, the Beatles 'performed as a group, sharing their music and lives with one another' (Jackson and Padgett, 1982). From 1967, however, and for a variety of reasons, the Beatles existed in name only, and solo-authored songs became more prevalent with one member of the group simply using the others as 'session musicians' or not using them at all.

Jackson and Padgett argued that songs written prior to 1967 should reflect no differences in effort between individually and co-written songs because, regardless of authorship, they were always identifiable. Beyond 1967, however, with the increase in identifiability and individuality, social loafing should be evident in the few songs that were the result of genuine collaboration. Thus, the researchers predicted that post-1967 songs written by either Lennon or McCartney would reflect greater effort than songs which were a result of genuine collaboration between them.

Jackson and Padgett argued that one plausible measure of the effort put into a song was the quality of the finished product. The researchers measured quality in two ways:

1   **whether or not a song was chosen as a single release (the argument being that songs chosen for single release are of higher quality) and**

2 **commercial success of a single release (measured in terms of its sales).**

Jackson and Padgett devised a points system which was applied to each of the 53 Lennon–McCartney compositions that were released as singles in America. The points system involved a combination of a song's chart position and its length of stay in the charts. Thus, a highly successful (i.e. number one) song with a long chart life (such as *Hey Jude*) received more points than a less successful song with a short chart life (such as *I'll Get You*).

On the basis of the lower quality of the post-1966 jointly authored songs, Jackson and Padgett concluded that from 1967 until the demise of the group, the Lennon–McCartney songwriting team loafed when they genuinely collaborated to write songs.

PREDICTIONS

There are various aspects of Jackson and Padgett's original research that could be tested here. These give rise to the following possible predictions.

* **There is a difference in the quality (as measured by the chart position and number of weeks in the chart) of individual authorship Lennon/McCartney songs and dual authorship Lennon–McCartney songs. (This would test for overall differences between individual and dual authorship songs, and explore the possibility of social loafing throughout the songwriting partnership of Lennon and McCartney.)**

* **There is a difference in the quality of individual authorship and dual authorship songs released after 1966. (Consistent with the reports of Beatles' biographers that collaboration was less successful after 1966, therefore social loafing may be evident in this period.)**

METHOD

It will be necessary to consult two documents:

1 **an encyclopedia of the Beatles that gives information about chart positions and chart life of Beatles' singles (e.g. *The Beatles Encyclopedia* by Bill Harry)**

2 **an extract from a 1981 interview with John Lennon in *Playboy* magazine – this is available in its entirety from the web. Just enter 'Lennon Playboy interview' in your favourite search engine. This information is also available in some encyclopaedia.**

First, you should go through the Beatles encyclopedia and make a list of all singles (excluding EPs). It is better to use singles released in the US (i.e. the *Billboard* charts – a trade publication which runs a Hot 100 chart of the best-selling singles in the US) as this generates more songs for analysis. The *Billboard* chart differs from the British version because it includes chart placings for the flipside of discs as well. Assign a score dependent on that single's chart position (1 = a score of 100, 2 = 99, 100 = 1 and so on). This should then be multiplied by the number representing the number of weeks that single spent in the chart (e.g. if a single reached number three in the charts and stayed in the charts 16 weeks, then its total quality score would be $98 \times 16 = 1568$. Where a song has re-entered the charts, the number of weeks from the re-entry should be added to the number of weeks from the original entry. The re-entry chart position should be ignored. If a single reaches number one in the chart, this should also be noted, as it will help with the rank ordering later on.

It will then be necessary to read the *Playboy* interview with John Lennon to establish authorship. *Any* contribution by the other member of the songwriting team (e.g. 'adding a line or two, or a 'few bars here and there') should be counted as joint authorship. The information in this interview can be combined with information gleaned from other sources to establish any degree of collaboration in the authorship of a particular song.

This information can then be transferred to a table as below. The author of each song (i.e. Lennon, McCartney or Lennon–McCartney) is denoted by '**L**', '**M**' or '**L/M**'). Songs authored by others are excluded from this list.

Table 20 Summary of Beatles' singles released in the US by authorship and chart success

	Main author	**Date of chart entry**	**Highest position**	**Weeks in chart**
I Want To Hold Your Hand	L/M	18.1.64	1(7)	15
She Loves You	L/M	25.1.64	1(2)	15
Please Please Me	L	1.2.64	3	13
I Saw Her Standing There	M	8.2.64	14	11

ANALYSING THE DATA

To test the first hypothesis, all the rated songs should be put in rank order according to their 'quality' score with the lowest score ranking 1, the second lowest 2 and so on. In the event of a tie with singles that have reached number one, the number of weeks that song spent at number one (noted in brackets) can be used to discriminate for rank position. The data could also be represented by means of a bar chart with the median 'quality' score on the vertical axis, and the authorship classifications (Pre-1967 joint, Pre-1967 single, Post-1967 joint, Post-1967 single) on the horizontal axis.

In order to determine whether there is a significant difference in the quality of single authored and joint authored songs, data should be analysed using a Mann–Whitney U test (see Chapter 10). To test the second hypothesis, using only the songs after 1966, the same analysis can be repeated.

DISCUSSION

Depending on your success with unravelling the various clues as to authorship of the different Beatles' singles, you may or may not have come to the same conclusions as Jackson and Padgett in their original study. There are a number of problems associated with this investigation. These include difficulties with the assessment of quality (necessary for the determination of social loafing), the accuracy of John Lennon's memory, the degree of collaboration for different songs (some were clearly joint efforts, others less so) and so on. Discussion should consider these problems, with practical solutions suggested as modifications.

Social psychologists have also established that social loafing is more likely in individualist cultures (where self-interest and individual rights are promoted) rather than in collectivist cultures (where the good of the group is considered more important than the good of the individual). You might explore the implications of this claim for the validity of any conclusions drawn from this study.

REFERENCES

Harry, B. (2000). *The Beatles Encyclopedia*. London: Virgin.

Jackson, J.M. and Padgett, V.R. (1982). 'With a little help from my friend: Social-loafing and the Lennon–McCartney songs'. *Personality and Social Psychology Bulletin*, 8, 672–677.

A B C D E F G H I J K L M N O P Q R S T U V W X Y Z

Attributional bias in the sports pages

INTRODUCTION

The self-serving bias refers to a tendency to attribute successful outcomes to dispositional (i.e. internal) factors and unsuccessful outcomes to situational (i.e. external) factors. If we do well in something we may well feel this success is due to our own ability or effort. If we do badly we may externalise the blame onto some other factor (like bad luck or dodgy textbooks). There are a number of reasons why the self-serving bias might occur:

- **cognitive** explanations stress the fact that if we expect to succeed we are more likely to relate success to our own efforts and externalise failure as being due to some other cause

- **motivational** explanations stress the need to feel good about ourselves and preserve a positive self-esteem. The self-serving bias allows us to preserve our sometimes fragile sense of self-worth

- **impression management** explanations see the self-serving bias operating because of our need to project an impression of competence and hard work. Failure may threaten this preferred image, therefore it is externalised.

Classic examples of the self-serving bias can be found every Monday in the sports pages of the national newspapers. Football teams frequently lose because of poor refereeing, indifferent support or the state of the pitch, but rarely because they weren't good enough or didn't try hard enough!

This study takes the form of a content analysis of the sports pages of newspapers. More specifically it is an investigation to study whether there is evidence of a 'self-serving bias' among football managers and players when explaining the reasons for their team's performance in a previous game. The self-serving bias is defined as 'the tendency to view one's successes as stemming from internal factors and one's failures as stemming from external factors'.

The project is based on the work of Lau and Russell (1980), who studied 33 major American football and baseball events reported in the daily newspapers during the autumn of 1977. Lau and Russell discovered a number of interesting biases in their analysis of the attributions made by players and coaches. Attributional statements made by members of the winning side were far more likely to be 'internal' (i.e. success was more likely to have been attributed to ability or effort of the victors). Members of the losing side, however, were as likely to attribute their defeat to factors outside of their control (e.g. the ability of the opposition, weather conditions or just plain bad luck). Lau and Russell also found that the more 'ego-involved' the person making the attribution (i.e. the importance of the outcome to preserve their own self-esteem) the more likely they were to employ the self-serving bias. Coaches and players, for example, were more likely to make an internal attribution after victory than were sportswriters.

Lau and Russell further predicted that expected outcomes would be more likely to result in internal attributions, whereas unexpected outcomes should result in more external attributions being made. Their findings did not, however, support this hypothesis.

PREDICTIONS

The actual predictions chosen will reflect which aspect of this study you choose to work on. Lau and Russell explored three main areas in which the self-serving bias might be evident:

- **attributions from managers and players concerning success and failure**

- **attributions from managers and players (closer ego-involvement) compared to sportswriters (less ego-involvement)**

- **attributions from managers and players concerning expected and unexpected results (this can be checked by comparing actual results with predicted results in newspapers or bookmakers).**

The most straightforward of these predictions is likely to be the first, although should time (and interest) allow, you might explore the latter two as well. Based on Lau and Russell's findings you might generate a directional hypothesis, but as their research was based on US sports events, and allowing for the fact that there may be important cultural differences (e.g. humility), a non-directional hypothesis might be safer.

METHOD

The first stage of your study is to gather together suitable data. The Monday newspapers (during the football season) are probably the best source of information. You will need to scour football reports looking for quotations about the match just played. You should only select quotations from managers and players (assuming you are testing the first hypothesis) and only from matches where there has been a definite outcome (i.e. do not include matches that were drawn). For a quote to be suitable, there are three main criteria:

- **the person giving the quote must be a player or manager**
- **the quote must be about his team's performance in a match they had either just won or lost**
- **the quote must contain some explanation for why his team had won or lost.**

Don't be overly selective at this stage (i.e. don't just pick attributional quotes that support your hypothesis) and be prepared to check the papers for quite a few weeks until you have enough. How many you select depends on how thorough you want to be and how much time you have available, but 40 would appear to be a minimum. This is where working as part of a group pays off, but check you aren't using the same quote from different newspapers!

Having collected all your quotations together, you must now code them as either success (the attributor's team won) or failure (the attributor's team lost). Next you need to code the locus of causality (technical term for whether they saw the outcome as caused by internal or external factors). Internal reasons are the ability or effort of their own team, external reasons are the ability or effort of the opposition, injuries, bad refereeing, the weather, luck, etc.

The following examples give you an idea of what you might be looking for.

- **Liverpool manager after his team had won:**

  'Michael [Michael Owen, a Liverpool player] was quite magnificent today, and that was the difference between the teams.'

  The Liverpool manager attributes the reason for his team's victory to the ability of one particular Liverpool player, therefore this would be coded as success-internal.

- **Manchester United manager after his team had won:**

  'Maybe we didn't deserve to win, we were second best for much of the game, but in the end they all count.'

  The Manchester United manager acknowledges that his team were lucky to win, therefore this would be coded as success-external.

- **Wimbledon manager after his team had lost:**

  'You don't win matches when you don't defend well, and we didn't.'

Here the failure of his team is being attributed to their own lack of ability and/or effort, therefore would be coded as **failure-internal**.

• Grimsby manager after his team had lost:

'I thought 4–1 was harsh on us, but Blackburn [the opposition] are a class act. They have half a dozen genuine Premiership players and there are not many of those in this league.'

Despite feeling that the score was a little harsh, the Grimsby manager attributes his team's loss to the ability of the opposition, therefore this would be coded as **failure-external**.

ANALYSING THE DATA

Scoring the data is a fairly straightforward process. For each statement collected, you need to establish two things. First, did the person's team win (coded as success) or lose (coded as failure). Second, did the person attribute this outcome to internal or external factors. This should enable you to construct a table similar to the one below:

Table 21 Contingency table for outcome of game and locus of causality

| | | Locus of causality | |
		Internal attribution	External attribution
Outcome	Success	15	6
	Failure	11	18

This table can then be used to carry out a chi-square test of association (see Chapter 10) in order to determine whether there is support for your predicted self-serving bias. You might also represent this data in the form of a bar chart.

DISCUSSION POINTS

There are a number of issues that arise as a result of this study, although the actual structure of your discussion section will depend largely on the particular specification you are following (see Chapters 12–15). You might, for example, discuss your findings in the light of your aims or hypotheses, compare your findings with those of Lau and Russell, and consider whether there is evidence for any of the explanations of the self-serving bias given in the introduction.

There are, of course, limitations to this study, not least of which is the possible difference between public and private attributions. Most football clubs now have their own websites, and these are a good place to tap into the thoughts of managers and players about recent performances. Although this study is restricted to the study of self-serving bias in sport, there may well be other areas that warrant investigation, or important implications of this research for mental health and self-development.

REFERENCES

Lau, R.R. and Russell, D. (1980). 'Attributions in the sports pages'. *Journal of Personality and Social Psychology,* 39, 29–38.

McIlveen, R. (1992). 'An investigation of attributional bias in a real world setting'. In R. McIlveen, L. Higgins and A. Wadeley (Eds), *BPS Manual of Psychology Practicals* (1992), Leicester: BPS Books.

Gender differences in the aggressive behaviour of schoolchildren

INTRODUCTION

Studies of bullying have noted that the playground is a place of particularly intense social interaction and often strong physical activity. Bullies frequently intimidate their victims more often in contexts where adults are rarely present, and where children play in a free way. In a study of primary school pupils in England, researchers found that children were bullied in the playground more than anywhere else (Whitney and Smith, 1993). The one finding that emerges consistently from research is the difference between males and females in their levels of involvement in violence, attitudes toward violence, and their responsiveness to the messages in violence prevention programmes. These differences appear to be rooted in cultural and social influences rather than the physiological make-up of boys and girls. Boys, conditioned by society to value power and dominance while avoiding any outward display of emotions other than anger, find it hard to accept anti-violence messages that are often directly opposed to their cultural conditioning. It is interesting to note that bullying tends to be manifested in different ways for boys and girls. Girls are more likely to be involved in verbal and indirect aggression while that involving boys is more often physical (Rivers and Smith, 1994).

A substantial amount of research has been conducted regarding the ways in which children acquire these so-called gender appropriate behaviours. According to Bandura (1969), social learning theory indicates that children learn their appropriate sex roles through observing the actions of others, as well as being either rewarded or punished for acting appropriately or inappropriately. That is to say that children learn personality and behaviour patterns through the imitation of their own parents' attitudes and behaviours. Television may teach children a great deal about sex-typed behaviours, simply because it brings an abundance of readily observable models into the child's own home. However, it is important to acknowledge that television programming is not the only source of gender-appropriate examples of behaviour. More often than not, normal social interaction between friends will reinforce what is regarded as appropriate behaviour for boys and girls.

This study explores whether gender differences *are* evident in the playground behaviour of boys and girls. It also offers an opportunity (for the more ambitious researcher) to investigate some of the different interactions that provoke bullying behaviour, therefore the study has potentially important implications for our understanding of this worrying phenomenon. The use of a naturalistic observation method allows us to record information about what happens in the playground (where children are less constrained), particularly in the interactions between peers.

Adopting a naturalistic observational approach to the study of gender differences in aggressive behaviour has several advantages. First, the school playground is an ideal location for studying peer interactions in their natural settings, with children free to choose their play partners and activities. Second, the playground offers an opportunity to study children of mixed age and sex (thus affording the opportunity to study different types of interactions) without the direct constraints of adult supervision. This has important implications for gaining insights into bullying.

PREDICTIONS

There is considerable research evidence to suggest that boys will display more physical aggression than girls, and girls more verbal aggression or indirect aggression than boys. This might generate a number of related hypotheses, of which you might choose one or more than one. For example, the following predictions might be tested.

- **There is a gender difference in the overall incidence of aggressive behaviours among primary age children in a playground setting.**

(This might be non-directional as it takes account of all types of aggression.)

- Primary age boys show a higher incidence of physically aggressive behaviours in a playground setting than do girls.

- Primary age girls show a higher incidence of verbally aggressive behaviours in a playground setting than do boys.

- Primary age girls show a higher incidence of indirect aggressive behaviours in a playground setting than do boys. (Indirect aggressive behaviour might be demonstrated by saying nasty things about someone else rather than saying nasty things to someone else.)

METHOD

Opportunity (i.e. school co-operation) may well determine the most appropriate age group to study, but this investigation works just as well for younger schoolchildren as for older. Ideally, observations should take place over a number of visits to the school, for two main reasons. First, a period of acclimatisation to the children is necessary, so that the presence of a stranger does not inhibit their behaviour. This will allow unobtrusive observations to take place. Second, several unobtrusive visits allow more observations, and therefore a more appropriate number of children can be studied. If the investigation is being carried out as a group project, then each member of the group could study a smaller number of children over more observational periods, and the results combined. Ideally, equal numbers of boys and girls should be used for the investigation, with each observer aiming to observe an equal number of boys and girls.

The observational procedure to be used is a type of event sampling, in which the time period during which observations are to be made is divided into intervals (e.g. 15-, 30-second or longer intervals). If a scorable behaviour (e.g. a display of physical or verbal aggression) occurs during this period, it is recorded. The presence or absence of the behaviour is the only aspect recorded, not the number of times it occurs during that period. Thus, if during a 30-second period the behaviour occurs six times, it is entered in the score sheet only once. It is suggested that each child is observed for five minutes in total, i.e. ten 30-second periods overall, or twenty 15-second periods. As each behaviour can be recorded only once in each observational period, there will be a maximum score of 20 for each behaviour.

The data can be recorded on a table such as the one below:

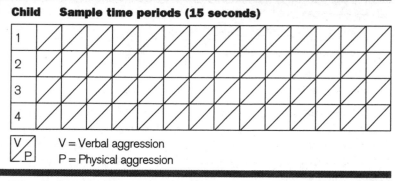

Child   Sample time periods (15 seconds)

V = Verbal aggression
P = Physical aggression

This will yield a total physical aggression score and a total verbal aggression score for each child observed (assuming that is the hypothesis being tested). You will, of course, need to note down whether the child is male or female.

You should also be aware of the particular ethical problems involved in school-children acting as participants in psychological investigations. Legal requirements for the protection of children place restrictions on the people who are allowed access to children in schools. Furthermore, parental consent may be necessary before studying those under 16 years of age in school. It is vital, therefore, that you consult your teacher well in advance of conducting this study, and they will advise you how best to approach the school or schools concerned.

ANALYSING THE DATA

The actual data presentation depends on the hypothesis being tested. For the first of the hypotheses suggested earlier ('There is a gender difference in the overall incidence of aggressive behaviours among primary age children in a playground setting'), a table such as the one below might be used.

Table 22 Mean number of 15-second periods in which target behaviour occurred

Behaviour category	Boys (n = ?)	Girls (n = ?)
Physical aggression		
Verbal aggression		
Indirect aggression		
Total aggressive acts		

These results can also be presented in the form of simple bar charts, so that visual analysis can take place. Does there appear to be any gender difference in the overall incidence of aggression? Is there any gender difference in the incidence of physical aggression or in the incidence of verbal aggression? Which gender appears the more aggressive for each of these types of aggressive behaviour?

In order to test whether there is a significant difference between the genders for three conditions (total aggressive acts, physically aggressive behaviour, verbally aggressive behaviour), it is necessary to carry out a statistical test. As each child will yield a total score for aggressive behaviour under each condition, we can compare the scores of each gender by examining the rank positions of males and females by using Mann–Whitney U tests (see Chapter 10).

DISCUSSION POINTS

The outcome of your statistical test(s) will determine whether the null hypotheses are to be retained or rejected for each of the investigative hypotheses, and this will give you the opportunity to compare your findings with those of other researchers in the field (e.g. Rivers and Smith, 1994).

The nature of this research raises a number of questions relating to methodology. Could these differences between the genders be a reflection of consistent patterns of aggression within the genders, or alternatively might they be due to a few individuals behaving aggressively? Individual differences within the genders could be a very important factor.

Most studies in this area have concentrated on measuring physical aggression, the demonstration of which is fairly obvious even to the casual observer. Observing verbal aggression, or indirect aggression is a far trickier exercise, given its often more subtle form. What sorts of problems were encountered in the measurement of these more subtle forms of aggression, and how might a researcher attempt to overcome such difficulties?

If pupils from more than one school are observed, there is the possibility of variables being confounded by background and situation, or by the constraints placed by individual teachers. Aggressive behaviour is often situation-specific, and its expression within a particular situation may have a developmental history which is unknown to the observer.

As in every observational study, there is the possibility of participant reactivity, in that children may react to the presence of the observer by responding either in a more inhibited or more exhibitionist manner. To overcome such problems is a skill in itself, so consideration should be given to how this study might have been improved in that respect, and how future studies in the area might be carried out more successfully.

This research might be usefully extended in many different ways, to take account of such factors as intra- and inter-sexual aggression and age differences in aggressive behaviour. What are the implications of research such as this? Does it give you any insights into the nature of bullying for example, or suggest ways in which such behaviour might be reduced?

REFERENCES

Cardwell, M.C. (1992). 'Gender differences in the aggressive behaviour of schoolchildren'. In R. McIlveen, L. Higgins and A.Wadeley (Eds), *BPS Manual of Psychology Practicals* (1992), Leicester: BPS Books.

Rivers, I. and Smith, P.K. (1994). 'Types of bullying behaviour and their correlates'. *Aggressive Behavior*, 20, 359–368.

Whitney, I. and Smith, P.K. (1993). 'A survey of the nature and the extent of bullying in junior, middle and secondary schools'. *Educational Research*, 35, 3–25.

The effects of ageing on cognition

INTRODUCTION

Ageing is associated with a generalised slowing of virtually all forms of information processing and this slowing affects memory performance as well. There are a number of theories about why memory tends to get worse with age. One proposal is that ageing impairs the retrieval system, thus older people have no problem storing information, but experience more difficulty than younger people when trying to retrieve it (Parkin, 1987). A general theme of ageing research is that age-related declines in memory functioning tend to increase as the environmental support provided by the task decreases. Memory tasks such as free recall (e.g. 'Recall the ten items shown earlier') provide little support for the retrieval processes required to perform the task. Recognition memory measures, on the other hand (e.g. 'was one of the items a toothbrush') provide more support in that they provide a cue for retrieval. Age-related declines in memory performance are more evident in recall tasks, which involve self-directed retrieval, rather than in recognition tasks, although a decline is often observed in recognition as well. An alternative explanation to the memory difficulties experienced in old age is to see these difficulties as a form of encoding deficit whereby problems in later recall and recognition can be explained by an organisational deficit during the encoding process. One way in which older people may experience this organisational deficit is through an inability to remember peripheral information about an event. Put simply, older people may have fewer resources available to them when learning new information. They may, for example, be able to remember the *details* of an event, but be less clear about the context in which the event occurred.

The study is based on the work of Cohen and Faulkner (1989) who investigated the idea that there would be age-related differences in people's ability to remember the context of a memorised event. They devised a method to test people's ability to remember whether they had watched an activity being performed, imagined it being performed, or actually carried it out for themselves. To do this they used small, everyday objects (e.g. pencil, clothes peg), and devised a number of simple actions to occur between pairs of these objects (e.g. clip the clothes peg around the pencil). Participants were either asked to carry out the action themselves, watch the researcher carrying out the action, or imagine it being carried out. After a short intervening delay, participants were given a list of activities (including some new to the participants which acted as distractors) and asked to indicate whether they had carried out, watched or imagined the activity being described.

Cohen and Faulkner tested three age groups (24–39, 60–68 and 72–83), and discovered that certain kinds of memory were worse in the older age groups. All participants made errors distinguishing between real and imagined actions, and in particular the oldest participants showed their weakest recall of activities they had been asked to imagine. In their research, Cohen and Faulkner (1989) found that older participants were more often misled by misleading information at the stage of retrieval and were also more confident in their erroneous responses than were younger participants.

If you are to attempt a replication or partial replication of this study, you should remember that this is not an opportunity for you to apply scientific principles to establish that your parents (or grandparents) have finally gone ga-ga. It should be conducted with the utmost care and sensitivity, and remember, its not how much you remember that's important, but the quality of your memories!

PREDICTIONS

This is quite an ambitious project, therefore you should be realistic when choosing your hypotheses. You may, for example, simply choose two age groups and predict a difference in overall memory performance between them. Alternatively you may test between the two age groups in terms of their ability to remember activities that *they* carried out, those they watched and so on. The study also gives you the opportunity to test for differences within age groups for different kinds of memory (e.g. real and imagined events). Your advance reading for this investigation will also tell you whether a directional or non-directional hypothesis is more appropriate for the particular relationship between age and memory that you have chosen to study.

METHOD

The method used will obviously depend very much on the particular hypotheses you have chosen for the study. You may, for example, choose young people of your own age group (assuming a range of 18–45 for example) and compare them to an older age group (such as 60–80). Either way, the actual procedure to be adopted is pretty much the same across all the different comparisons possible.

1   **Collect together 60 small everyday objects (avoiding objects that would be familiar to one gender but not to the other). Construct a 6 × 10 grid on card (giving a total of 60 squares) on which these items can be placed.**

2   **Construct a list of 30 different activities that involve two of the items on the grid. For example, you may have 'put the penny in the egg-cup' and 'wrap the string around the spoon'. Don't use obvious connections here (such as 'put the egg in the egg-cup'). Put these onto cards and shuffle them.**

3   **Randomly assign these activity statements to one of three conditions:**

   • **10 actions that your participants will perform themselves**

   • **10 actions they will watch you perform**

   • **10 actions you will ask them to imagine doing.**

4   **Devise a further 10 activity statements that you will not use during this part of the experiment, but will act as distractors during the later retrieval process.**

5   **Decide on a suitable distractor task (such as counting backwards in threes from 1000 to prevent rehearsal). This should last about 10 minutes.**

6   **Give your participants a sheet which contains the 40 activity statements (30 they had experienced plus the 10 distractors) on**

which they should indicate (by ticking the appropriate category) whether they had performed, watched, imagined or not experienced the activity (i.e. a non-event). Count up the number they got right in each category (remember, there will be a maximum of 10 for each category).

Activity	Performed	Watched	Imagined	Non-event
Put the penny in the egg-cup				
Wrap the string around the pencil				
Stick the needle into the rubber				
Put the paper-clip on the playing card				

ANALYSING THE DATA

There are lots of interesting and informative ways in which you can present the data from this study. Remember that visual presentation (in graphs or otherwise) should never be used as a substitute for verbal commentary on your data. It does, however, supplement other forms of presentation. Bar charts are a good way of showing the differences between the age groups for the four different categories of event, and can also be used for a visual analysis of differences *within* a particular age group.

For inferential analysis, you should carry out a test such as the Mann–Whitney *U* test (see Chapter 10) for each of the categories being compared across the two age groups. For example, if you have two age groups and four categories, you would carry out the four tests as below:

* age group 1 versus age group 2 – performed activities
* age group 1 versus age group 2 – watched activities
* age group 1 versus age group 2 – imagined activities
* age group 1 versus age group 2 – non-event activities

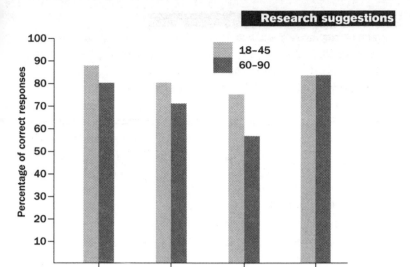

Percentage of correct responses across all categories for the two age groups

To test for differences within an age group on each of these categories, a suitable test would be the Wilcoxon test (see Chapter 10), with tests being carried out as follows:

- **age group 1, performed versus watched activities**
- **age group 1, performed versus imagined activities**
- **age group 1, performed versus non-event activities**
- **age group 1, watched versus imagined activities**
- **age group 1, watched versus non-event activities**
- **age group 1, imagined versus non-event activities**

The same list of analyses should then be carried out for the second age group. This is obviously a long and laborious process, but tests such as Mann–Whitney and Wilcoxon are fairly simple to carry out, and you will certainly have mastered their calculation at the end of it all. Remember, however, that the real skill of analysis comes from your ability to *interpret* these results and relate them back to your aims and hypotheses, so don't neglect this aspect of your results section.

DISCUSSION POINTS

As with all the suggested investigations in this chapter, there is a requirement to discuss your findings within the constraints and individual requirements imposed by the specification that you are following. As a general approach, however, you should consider how these findings relate back to your earlier aims and hypotheses, how they fit in with the research context, particularly in respect to the claims made in the introduction to this investigation. You may well have found an age-related difference in performance, but you should consider whether this is explained only by considering the possible cognitive deficits of the older age group. Your participants may differ in many other ways (e.g. the demands made on their time, their motivation to carry out the investigation and perform as well as they could, and so on).

As with all investigations, they should, hopefully, have some relevance to life in the real world, and even possible applications for improving memory in old age. What are the implications of this study, and what avenues of further research has it prompted? You never know, you may just benefit from this research yourself one day ...

REFERENCES

Cohen, G. and Faulkner, D. (1989). 'The effects of ageing on perceived and generated memories'. In L.W. Poon, D.C. Rubin and B.A. Wilson (Eds), *Everyday Cognition in Later Life* (1989). Cambridge: Cambridge University Press.

Parkin, A.J. (1987). *Memory & Amnesia*. Oxford: Blackwell.

Wadeley, A.E. (2001). 'Can you remember? Studying the effects of ageing on cognition'. *Psychology Review*, 7, 1, 12–15.

As students frequently experience difficulty getting hold of information for their introduction section, the following websites offer invaluable access to research and other relevant information of direct relevance to this investigation:

Memory Web Connections (www.manchester.edu/Users/Facstaff/NEKelley/webmemor.htm) provides links to memory and ageing as well as tricks for improving memory and memory training.

A paper presented to the 1997 World Congress of Gerontology by Denise Park (University of Michigan) titled 'Ageing and Memory: Mechanism Underlying Age Differences in Performance' is also available online at www.cas.flinders.edu.au/iag/proceedings/proc0026.htm

A-Z Glossary of coursework terms

average: a measure or indication of what is typical or central in a set of scores. More exactly it is used in its mathematical sense, where, as the mean, it is calculated by dividing the sum of all the scores by the total number of scores.

bar chart: a way of graphically representing scores on some discrete variable. For example, we may want to represent the number of cars of different nationalities in the college car park. The resulting bar chart might look something like this.

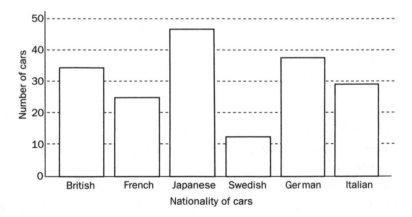

baseline: a point of comparison against which the effect of some treatment can be assessed. In experiments, the control group is commonly used as a baseline against which to assess the effectiveness of the independent variable.

biased sampling refers to the over-representation of one category of participant (males, females, students, people of a certain age, etc.) in a sample so that the sample fails to represent adequately the population from which it was taken.

ABCDEFGHIJKLMNOPQRSTUVWXYZ

bimodal distribution: a type of frequency distribution where there are two modes, i.e. two equally high points on the graph.

BPS: a common abbreviation of the British Psychological Society.

case study: an attempt to explore, in some considerable depth, the behaviour and experiences of an individual. Case studies involve detailed descriptions of those aspects of the behaviour which are of interest to the person carrying out the study as well as their interpretations of what they have found.

categorical variables are variables where differences between people are identified only by categories rather than by measurements along some kind of scale. In an experiment the independent variable (that is, the conditions of the experiment) is usually categorical.

cause and effect: a belief that a cause can be established for every event. In an experiment, the independent variable that is manipulated is hypothesised as the cause, and the resultant change in behaviour (the dependent variable) is the effect.

central tendency: a typical value in a set of scores, normally calculated as either the mean, median or mode. The nature of the data tends to determine which of these measures is the most appropriate to use.

chi-square test of association: a statistical test which assesses the association between two variables. For example, the test may assess whether there is an association between gender and newspaper preference, or whether an observed tendency for men to buy one type of paper and women another is likely to be mere coincidence.

confidentiality: an ethical requirement of both research and therapy, in which participants or clients have the right to expect that information gathered during the research or therapy session will not be made public without their consent.

consent: an ethical requirement which requires that all participants or clients should agree to the procedures which are to take place. Within a research context this also implies that participants should be free to withdraw from the study at any time without undue pressure being put upon them to continue.

content analysis: a general term which refers to the fact that sometimes people are not studied directly, but indirectly, through what they produce (political speeches, literary works and so on). It is possible to obtain some understanding of a person's psychological state or perhaps evidence of some more general behaviour within a culture by looking closely at the content of these products.

control group: in an experiment, a group of participants matched as closely as possible to the experimental group that does not receive the independent variable. If the performance of the experimental group is significantly different to that of the control group, the experimenter can attribute the difference to the effect of the independent variable.

correlation coefficient: a mathematical representation of the degree of relatedness of two sets of measurements. A coefficient of +1 indicates a perfect positive correlation, in that high values of one measure (such as height) might relate perfectly to high values of another (such as foot size). A coefficient of −1 indicates a perfect negative correlation (also known as an inverse relationship) in that high values of one measure (such as miles per hour) might relate perfectly to low values of the other (such as miles per gallon). A coefficient of 0 would indicate no relationship at all between the two sets of measurements.

counterbalancing: an experimental technique used to overcome order and practice effects. If experimental conditions are always carried out in the same order (condition A followed by condition B) then it makes it possible that participants might improve or get worse simply as a result of the order in which they carry out the two conditions (due to the effects of learning, fatigue, boredom, etc.).

data: information or measurements gathered during the course of a study. The interpretation of data allows the research psychologist to draw conclusions about the event under study.

debriefing: a post-experimental interview in which the experimenter tries to restore the participant to the same psychological state they were in when they entered the experiment. Debriefing is especially vital when participants have been deceived in any way during the experiment.

deception: the deliberate misleading of participants during a research study, either through telling them lies or by omitting to tell them some important detail of the research such that they are unable to give their full informed consent.

demand characteristic: any aspect of the experimental situation that prompts the participant to interpret the study in a specific way and adjust their behaviour accordingly. By adjusting their behaviour to what they see as the 'demands' of the experiment, participants introduce a bias that may contaminate the results of the study.

dependent variable: some aspect of behaviour that is affected by the action of the independent variable in an experiment. An experimental effect is produced if the independent variable causes a change in the dependent variable.

distribution: a graphical representation of the frequency with which certain scores are found. This can be represented in a number of different ways including histograms.

ecological validity refers to the degree to which the results of an investigation can be generalised beyond the immediate setting in which they were gathered to other settings and other situations. Something is only ecologically valid if it can be shown to occur outside of the immediate setting in which it was observed.

effect: literally, something that happens as a direct result of something else. In experiments, it is possible to establish a cause and effect relationship between two measured variables. For example, if giving alcohol to participants causes them to fall over, then the falling over is the effect.

empirical research refers to research that results in the collection, analysis and evaluation of data.

ethics: a consideration of what is acceptable or right behaviour in the pursuit of a particular personal or scientific goal. The publication of clear guidelines (for example those produced by the British Psychological Society) ensures that research is carried out in a way that is in the best interests of the participants, and is also morally defensible to those outside the research context. These guidelines include reference to the importance of informed consent and the avoidance of deception. Simple rule following may not, however, always produce the most ethically correct research.

event sampling: an aspect of observational studies, where an event is recorded every time it occurs. For example, if we were recording the intricacies of a football match, we might record every time a particular player passed the ball, tackled, hurled abuse at the referee and so on. Event sampling rarely involves more than a simple recording of the incidence (i.e. whether it occurred or not, and if so how many times) of a particular behaviour.

ex post facto study: a type of research study in which the independent variable is some aspect of the participant (such as their age, gender, political persuasion or whatever). As the researcher has no control over the independent variable in that s/he cannot manipulate it, the independent variable can only be varied by selecting participants that differ in the chosen feature (e.g. different age groups). Because manipulation of the independent variable is not possible, and participants cannot be randomly assigned to different conditions (such as age groups) the relationship between independent variable and dependent variable cannot be established as a causal one. Thus we may say that people of different age groups perform differently in some way, but we cannot say that these differences in behaviour were caused by age.

experiment: an experiment involves the manipulation of an independent variable in order to see its effect on a dependent variable. In simple terms, an experimenter will manipulate some aspect of a situation and then observe the effect that this has on some aspect of behaviour.

experimental designs: procedures used to control for the influence of participant variables in an experiment. There are three major types of experimental design.

- **The repeated measures design – all participants take part in all conditions.**

- **Matched subjects (participants) design – an attempt is made to relate the participants in some way. One of each matched pair participates in one condition of the study while the second participates in the other condition.**

- **The independent subjects (participants) design – participants are randomly allocated to different conditions.**

experimental group: those participants in an experiment who receive the experimental treatment level of the independent variable under study.

experimenter effect refers to some aspect of the experimenter's make-up or of their behaviour that has an effect on the behaviour of the participant in an investigation. Through unintentional bias during the recording of data, and the general procedural details of the investigation, researchers may also obtain results that are consistent with their expectations.

external validity is the ability to generalise results obtained in a laboratory study to other settings and other participants.

Eysenck Personality Inventory (EPI): a way of measuring personality along the dimensions of extraversion–intraversion, and neuroticism–stability. Clients are asked a series of questions such as 'Do you tend to enjoy yourself at parties?' By responding 'Yes' or 'No' to these questions, the person filling out the inventory is providing information for the psychologist to construct a profile which will give them a score for extraversion and for neuroticism. As some people who fill out the inventory may fake their answers and try to respond in a way that is socially desirable, the inventory also includes a lie scale of questions that can only be answered in one way. If the client scores over a certain number on the lie scale, the overall test results are discarded.

field studies: literally any piece of research that takes place outside of the laboratory, and within the context in which a behaviour normally occurs.

forced-choice item refers to any test where respondents have to choose one of a number of alternative responses. For example, they may be asked to choose between two statements, neither of which really reflects their true feelings. Although this may seem like a pointless thing to ask people to do, it does have the advantage that it largely overcomes the tendency to produce socially desirable responses and enables the investigator to look for consistent trends in the responses given.

frequency graph: a graphical representation of how often certain events or scores occur. Frequency distributions can be represented in a number of different ways including histograms.

histogram: a type of frequency distribution where the number of scores in each category is represented by a vertical column.

hypothesis: a claim about the world. It is a statement of what you believe to be true. The fundamental requirement of any hypothesis is that it can be tested against reality (i.e. is it true or not?) and can then be supported or rejected. To test our hypothesis we first assume that there is no difference between the populations from which the samples were taken. This is known as the null hypothesis (H_0). The research hypothesis is often called the 'alternative hypothesis'.

independent variable: some aspect of the experimental situation that is directly manipulated by the experimenter in order to see if it causes a change in some other behaviour (the dependent variable), for example allocating participants to either a drug or placebo condition (independent variable) in order to measure any change in the intensity of their anxiety (dependent variable).

inter-rater reliability refers to the need to assess the degree to which two or more observers agree on the classification or scoring of the behaviour being studied. The more that observers agree the higher is the inter-rater reliability.

levels of measurement refers to the way in which a variable is measured in psychological research investigations. The different levels of measurement simply extract different types of information depending on the amount of information available in the data, and the nature of the measuring instrument being used. The main levels are given below.

- **Nominal data – grouped into categories.**
- **Ordinal data – in the form of ratings or ranks.**
- **Interval data – the measurement scale being used has fixed units of measurement (such as an inch, a second, etc.) but the lack of a real zero value means that different scores cannot be taken as proportions of each other.**
- **Ratio data – like interval data, but zero actually means zero, and proportional comparisons become meaningful. A distance of 2 miles is twice as far as a distance of 1 mile.**

Likert scale: an attitudinal measurement scale which measures an individual's agreement or disagreement with attitude statements such as 'Psychologists hold the answers to all life's problems'. There are usually five different levels of agreement or disagreement, going from 'Strongly agree' through 'Undecided/neutral' to 'Strongly disagree'.

Mann–Whitney *U* test: a distribution-free statistical test that is used on ranked data collected from independent samples designs.

matching: a procedure in experimental design whereby participants in one condition are matched with participants in another in terms of anything that might have an effect on the dependent variable. This might be age, sex or a myriad of other factors.

mean: the arithmetic average calculated by dividing the total of all scores added together by the number of scores, e.g. 3, 5, 6, 3, 3: mean = 4.

measure of central tendency: a measurement that provides some sort of typical value in a set of scores. The mean is perhaps the most sensitive of the measures in that a change in any single score will change the value of the mean. The median and the mode would usually be unaffected however.

measure of dispersion: a measurement of the spread or variability in a set of scores. Although the measure of central tendency tells us what a typical score is in a set of scores, it does not tell us how far the other scores are spread around that central score. Measures of dispersion add that information.

median: the middle value in a set of scores when they are placed in a rank order, e.g. 3, 3, 3, 5, 6: median = 3.

mode: the most frequently occurring value in a set of scores, e.g. 3, 3, 3̲, 5, 6: mode = 3.

naturalistic observation: a type of investigation that is characterised by (a) the observer not attempting to manipulate any aspect of the situation, but merely watchiing and recording (b) the observations do not take place in the artificial environment of the laboratory but in the natural settings in which we would normally find that behaviour. There are two main types of observational technique: participant observation and non-participant observation. In the former, the observer will join in with the activities of a group in order to gain a greater insight and depth of understanding of their behaviour. In the latter technique, the observer endeavours to remain unobtrusive and records details of an individual's or group's behaviour, normally without the participants being aware of the observer's presence or the purposes of the investigation.

non-experimental approaches: simply any investigative approach that does not qualify by definition as an experiment. An experiment is traditionally defined as a procedure where the investigator manipulates some aspect of a situation in order to observe the effects of that manipulation. In the absence of that manipulation an investigation would be considered to be 'non-experimental'. Some types of experiment (e.g. natural experiments) do not have this direct manipulation as a feature so are regarded as 'quasi-experiments'. Examples of non-experimental approaches in psychology would include the observational method, case studies and any where existing differences between groups (e.g. extrovert and introvert) are investigated.

Arguments about which method is best, experimental or non-experimental, are pretty futile, as each offers different advantages to the researcher. Experiments generally offer greater control and an ability to make statements about cause and effect. Non-experimental methods, on the other hand, tend to offer insights derived from more life-like situations.

non-participant observation: a type of observational technique where the researcher observes the behaviour of an individual or group without intruding into the situation being studied. (See *naturalistic observation*.)

normal distribution refers to the symmetrical, bell-shaped curve that might be produced when a set of scores is represented on a frequency graph.

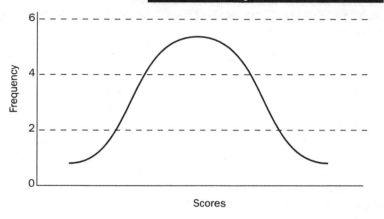

In a normal distribution, the majority of scores are clustered around a mid point with the lower and higher scores being less frequent towards the end of the distribution. These 'tails' of the distribution extend in both directions and theoretically never touch the *x* (horizontal) axis.

null hypothesis: when investigating our alternative hypothesis, we first assume that there is no difference between the populations from which the samples were taken. This is known as the null hypothesis (H_0) and would be written formally as in this example: 'The number of errors made on a letter cancellation task for the music group is equal to the number of errors made on a letter cancellation task for the silence group'. We make this assumption then calculate the probability that our two samples would differ as they did if this were true. If this probability comes out as very low (lower than 0.05) then we reject the null hypothesis and accept, provisionally, the alternative hypothesis (H_1).

observation: a very general term used to describe any situation where the participant is not constrained or manipulated in any way, and the observer records the behaviour that is exhibited by the participant. The term 'observation' may be used as a technique for gathering data (i.e. we observe somebody doing something) or as the design of a study. It is this second meaning of the term that leads to great variety of usage. To give a precise definition of the term observation means contrasting it with an experimental study. In an observation there is usually no manipulation of an independent variable. There are many different types of study that would be classified as 'observational' under this definition. The table below gives some of the commonest categories:

Controlled observation	Participants are observed in an environment which is, to some degree, under the control of the observer
Naturalistic observation	Behaviour is studied within its natural context e.g. children are observed whilst playing in a school playground
Participant and non-participant observation	An observer participates in the group being studied (participant) or observes from outside the group and tries not to be intrusive in any way (non-participant)
Structured observation	Observation is guided by the use of specific observational categories, e.g. an event may be recorded every time it happens (event sampling) or by the frequency of it happening within specific time periods (time sampling)

observer bias: the tendency for observers who are aware of the hypothesis under test to see and record what might be expected rather than what actually happens. To guard against this we can use observers who have no knowledge of the predictions being made.

open-ended questions: a technique used in unstructured interviews and surveys, where the questioner asks the respondent a question and the respondent can answer in any way they wish. This type of question gives a great deal more depth and insight into participants' behaviour, but it is difficult to quantify for later analysis.

operational definition: an aspect of effective scientific methodology, operational definitions are precise definitions of the terms used in studies. For example, in an experiment to test the effect of arousal on performance, we would need to know exactly what sort of arousal and how we would measure it. We would also need to know what type of performance we were suggesting that arousal affected, and how we would measure that. General aspects of behaviour like 'confidence' or even 'aggression' are usually quite hard to define. An operational definition is a definition in terms of the *operations* performed to measure the construct, e.g. intelligence = score on an IQ test; hungry = food-deprived by 4 hours. However, you must create suitable operational definitions before you can even think about data gathering for your project. Without the use of precise definitions, it is difficult to be anything but vague in scientific research, and it makes replication of research almost impossible.

order effect refers to the fact that research participants may perform differently on the different conditions in an experiment simply because of the order in which they do them. Participants may become tired, more or less tense, hungry, fed up, etc. We normally try to minimise the influence of order effects by ensuring that participants do not all perform the different conditions in the same order.

participant: a term used to describe those people who are studied and who contribute data in a research investigation. The term is now more favoured than the earlier term 'subject' which, it was felt, depersonalised the people who took part in studies. The term 'subject' is now used almost exclusively to refer to non-human animals.

Pearson's product moment test: a test of correlation that requires either interval or ratio data (see *levels of measurement*) which is in the form of related pairs of scores.

personality inventory: a test that is designed to measure personality characteristics. The Eysenck Personality Inventory (EPI) based on the personality theory of H.J. Eysenck measures personality along the dimensions of neuroticism–stability and extraversion–intraversion.

pilot study: an initial run-through of the procedures to be used in an experiment. By selecting a few participants and trying out the experiment on them we can save time and money on later mistakes. The pilot study is a good way of finding out whether the whole thing is likely to work as we planned it, and also if there are any floor or ceiling effects.

population: a group of people who are the focus of a research study and to which the results would apply. It is generally inappropriate to study an entire population (for example, all the students in a college, or all 16–19-year-olds in Liverpool) so a representative sample is studied instead.

practice effect: within an experiment, any improvement in performance over the different conditions of the experiment that might be attributed not to the independent variable under study, but to the learning that takes place when the same task is attempted on more than one occasion. If we were trying to measure how well participants perform a task under two different conditions, we must face the possibility that some of this difference would be inevitable because of the simple fact that they are by now familiar with the task. Provided that the practice effects are not too large, we can compensate for them by ensuring that half of the participants perform the conditions in the opposite order to the others (known as counterbalancing). If the effects are

A B C D E F G H I J K L M N O P Q R S T U V W X Y Z

large however, it would be necessary to use different participants in the different conditions of the experiment.

probability: a statement of how likely it is that something will happen. This is expressed as a number between 1 (certainty) and 0 (impossibility). A probability of 0.05 is conventionally used in psychological investigations as the appropriate point at which to reject the possibility that results are only differing because of sampling error. 0.05 is the probability of the difference or correlation occurring if the null hypothesis is true.

qualitative research: has developed largely out of dissatisfaction with the 'number crunching' approach of traditional experimental psychology. It is the belief of those who use qualitative methods that the conclusions which might be drawn from psychological research studies are always context-bound, i.e. they cannot really be generalised beyond the context in which they were gathered. Of particular importance in this context-specific view of the research process is the use of language, in other words 'what does this mean to you?' Qualitative research stresses the interpretation of language (through interviews and diaries, for example) rather that attempting simply to transform it into numbers. In this way, the researcher maintains a close focus on what is being said, and the context of expression. Case studies may be used so that one person can be studied in depth using this time-consuming approach.

quasi-experiment is a type of experiment where the experimenter does not directly influence the allocation of participants to the conditions under study, but makes use of existing divisions in terms of the conditions of interest. It also includes 'natural experiments' where the IV is not manipulated by the researcher.

questionnaire: see *surveys and interviews*.

random allocation refers to the way in which experimenters divide participants into the different experimental conditions such that there is no bias in the distribution of participant characteristics.

randomisation: a way of minimising order effects. The order in which participants tackle conditions is determined by random selection.

range: a measure of dispersion within a set of scores. It is calculated by subtracting the lowest score from the highest and adding 1; it gives an idea of the spread of the scores. The range is a rather simple descriptive statistic and is only of any real value when the scores are fairly closely bunched. If they are not, then it gives the impression of a uniformly even distribution of scores across the range when this is not the case.

ranks: putting a list of scores into a rank order with the lowest rank (i.e. 1) going to lowest value, e.g.

Student	Psychology essay scores	Rank
Radha	14	3
John	8	1
George	21	5
Dave	19	4
Rob	11	2

rating scale refers to the assessment of a person or behaviour along some scale. For example, schools often give ratings for effort and achievement in particular subjects when writing progress reports:

Student	Effort in science	Achievement
Chris	1	A
Scott	4	D
Paul	2	B
Lee	1	B
Adam	2	C

ratio scale: see *levels of measurement*.

reactivity: changes in the behaviour of people being observed that are due to the fact that they know they are being watched. The term refers to the fact that participants react to the presence of an observer and change their behaviour in one of a number of ways, e.g. by showing off, showing evaluation apprehension, trying harder, etc.

reliability: if a finding can be repeated it is described as being reliable. Within this general meaning of the term, it is also used more specifically within psychological assessment and research.

- For a research finding to be reliable it must be shown to exist on successive investigations under the same conditions (replication).

- For a psychometric assessment to be reliable it should have both internal and external reliability. Answers to a questionnaire or inventory may be checked to see if respondents answer all questions in the same way or if they contradict themselves. This is a measure of internal reliability. Responses may also be checked over a period of time to see if there is stability of measurement over time. If respondents give the same responses or obtain the same scores consistently over time, then the measure is said to have external reliability.

replication refers to whether a particular finding can be repeated with different people on different occasions. We are more likely to trust a research finding if it can be shown not to be a 'one-off'. Replication of a particular finding by other psychologists is vital in establishing a scientific theory.

representative sample: a group of participants that accurately represents the population under study. The sample may reflect the gender and age distributions of the underlying population as well as any other characteristics that, in the opinion of the investigator, might affect the outcome of the study. If the sample taken failed to represent adequately the population, it would be inappropriate to draw any conclusions from the sample about the population. (See *sampling*.)

research: a general term given to any attempt to study a problem through the collection and/or analysis of data. Psychologists more usually use the term to refer to an investigative process such as the experiment or the case study.

response bias: a tendency to respond in one particular way to a test item. Response bias is the tendency for a respondent to answer all questions (e.g. by ticking 'yes') in the same way, regardless of context.

robustness: a quality attributed to statistical tests that can function effectively in the calculation of probability despite the fact that assumptions surrounding their use have been compromised.

sample: a group of people that takes part in a research investigation and is presumed to be representative of the population from which it has been drawn.

sampling refers to the process by which research psychologists attempt to select a representative group from the population under study. As an entire population tends to be too large to work with, a smaller group of participants must act as a representative sample.

In an attempt to select a representative sample and thus avoid sampling bias (the over-representation of one category of participant in the sample), psychologists utilise a variety of sampling methods such as those given below.

- **Random sample – each member of the population under study stands the same chance of being selected.**

- **Stratified sample – the composition of the sample reflects the composition of the population, e.g. 30% males 70% females in the population determines that the sample shall contain a random selection of 30% females, 70% males.**

- **Quota sample – the researcher selects a quota of people roughly in proportion to their occurrence in the population (e.g. a quota of different age groups).**

- **Opportunity sample – roughly a case of selecting whoever is available at the time at that location.**

scattergram: a graphical representation of the correlation between two sets of measurements (for example, between IQ and total number of A level points achieved). In a linear correlation (i.e. where the points go in only one direction) a direction of bottom left to top right represents a positive correlation, whilst a direction of top left to bottom right indicates a negative correlation.

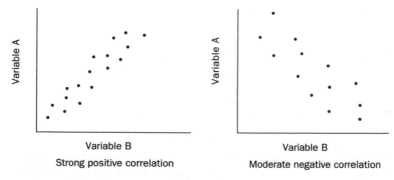

Strong positive correlation   Moderate negative correlation

significance: see *statistical significance*.

single-blind control: an experimental procedure used where participants do not know the independent variable being manipulated or which of the conditions they are in. The purpose of a single-blind procedure is to minimise the possibility that participants might alter their behaviour in order to produce what they believe is the most appropriate response.

single-subject (participant) experimental design: also known as $n = 1$ research, this involves using only one participant instead of a group of participants in an experimental study. This can provide useful early feedback about the action of the independent variable, and enables the experimenter to check the procedures to be used in the major study.

skewed distribution: a distribution of scores which, when plotted onto a graph, forms a distribution which has the majority of scores clumped toward one end or another. For example, if a test used in an experiment is too easy, most participants will do well (the ceiling effect) and the distribution this produces will be negatively skewed. If a test is too difficult, most participants will do badly (the floor effect) and the distribution this produces will be positively skewed.

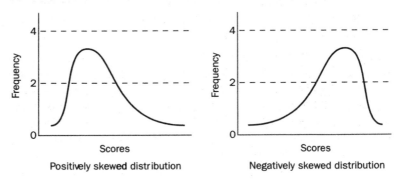

Positively skewed distribution   Negatively skewed distribution

Spearman's rho: a correlation which can be calculated from two sets of ranked data. Spearman's correlation is used with ordinal data (see *levels of measurement*) and produces a mathematical figure (the correlation coefficient) between +1 (a perfect positive correlation) and −1 (a perfect inverse or 'negative' correlation). A correlation of 0 indicates no relationship.

standard deviation: a statistical measure of the variation in a set of scores. The standard deviation gives a researcher an idea of how 'spread-out' a set of scores is around the mean value. With large data sets, between one standard deviation above and below the mean is where roughly 68% of all values lie.

standardised instructions: a set of instructions used in an experiment that is consistent in style, content and delivery across all conditions and participants of the experiment. As the instructions are often the only verbal interaction between the experimenter and the participant during the experimental session, it is important that what is said is the same for everyone, otherwise it adds another possible variable that can influence behaviour. Standardised instructions may be written down or presented on a computer monitor to ensure complete similarity across all participants.

standardised procedures refer to a fixed set of rules and procedures used in the administration and scoring of either an experiment or a psychometric test. It is important that standardised procedures are adhered to as even the smallest variations may have a greater impact on participant performance than the researcher is able to predict.

statistic: a mathematical calculation, which reflects the characteristics of a sample of behaviour or of the selected participants in a study. As used in psychological research, a statistic such as the mean or standard deviation that is calculated from a sample is generally assumed to represent the underlying characteristics of the population from which the sample has been drawn.

statistical significance: in a statistical significance test we assume the null hypothesis is true and calculate the probability of a difference occurring if this is so. If $p < 0.05$ we reject the null hypothesis and assume there is a real difference between the populations from which the two samples have been (randomly) drawn. At this point we accept that something is producing an effect, although because of the nature of psychological research, this 'something else' is not always certain. The fact that something is 'statistically significant' tells us that it is unlikely to have been caused by chance, but does not necessarily tell us that the result is of any particular significance.

surveys and interviews are techniques where investigators make use of questionnaires to obtain information about a particular area. Surveys are generally remote, in that respondents (people who complete the questionnaires) do not have an interviewer present, whereas interviews involve face-to-face interaction between the interviewer and the respondent. The investigator first defines an area of interest, e.g. people's attitude to television violence, and designs questions that will elicit information relevant to that topic. Interviewers are specially trained to deliver questions in a standardised way, that is without bias or encouragement to respondents to answer in a certain way. If interviewers cannot develop an appropriate rapport with their interviewees then questions may not be answered in an open and honest manner.

A
B
C
D
E
F
G
H
I
J
K
L
M
N
O
P
Q
R
S
T
U
V
W
X
Y
Z

time sampling involves brief periods of observation such that a number of individuals can be observed. For example, if we had to observe a group of 10 people over a one-hour period, we might observe each person for ten 30-second time samples, and build up some idea of the frequency and consistency of specific behaviour patterns.

two-tailed hypothesis: also known as a 'non-directional' hypothesis, this claims that there is a difference (or correlation, or association) between two populations, but does not state in which direction. So, we may predict that there will be a difference in performance between a group of people (the experimental group) receiving the independent variable and another group (the control group) who do not, but unless we actually say which group is likely to perform better, the hypothesis is two-tailed.

two-tailed test: when testing for statistical significance, a two-tailed statistical test is used when there is the possibility that results may occur in either predicted direction (as demonstrated in the non-directional or two-tailed hypothesis). A one-tailed test, on the other hand, is used only when the researcher is convinced (and expresses this in a directional or one-tailed hypothesis) that the results could go in one direction only. In practical terms, you would use the direction of your hypothesis to determine which set of critical values you would use when looking up whether the result of a statistical test is significant or not at the predetermined level.

type 1 error: an error made following statistical analysis if the null hypothesis is rejected when it is true. There are a number of reasons for making a type 1 error, but the commonest is through the adoption of a significance level that is not stringent enough, for example choosing to reject the null hypothesis at the $p = 0.10$ level rather than the more customary $p = 0.05$ level. That is considered unacceptably high, as too many type 1 errors are likely to occur.

type 2 error: an error made following statistical analysis if the null hypothesis is retained when it is false. The commonest reason for this type of error is if the significance level adopted is too stringent, for example choosing not to reject the null hypothesis at the customary $p = 0.05$ level, and holding out until the 0.01 level instead. In this case the probability of the difference occurring under the null hypothesis might be considered low enough at the $p = 0.05$ level, therefore to insist on a $p = 0.01$ level might be seen as unnecessarily stringent.

validity refers to the confidence that we may have that a test, measurement or experimental manipulation is actually doing the job it has been designed to do. This very general term is used in many different ways within psychology. Within an experiment, it is possible to assess:

- **internal validity** – was the observed effect really a product of the experimental manipulation? In Milgram's obedience to authority studies, conclusions regarding the effect of authority would have been invalid if the participants had not believed they had really been giving electric shocks

- **external validity** – even if the experiment has worked, the results may not apply to other people and to other situations. Social psychology experiments are often criticised for their reliance on American undergraduates and their use of the laboratory as a context for the research (see also *ecological validity*).

variable: literally anything whose value is free to change. Thus, in a test of intelligence, intellectual ability is the variable. In an experiment to test the effects of loud music on mental arithmetic, the loudness of the music is the variable. Variables are usefully divided into independent variables, dependent variables and extraneous variables when used in an experimental design.

variance: a measure of dispersion in a set of scores. That is, it gives us some indication of the amount of variation in those scores. The bigger the variance, the more the scores are spread around the mean rather than all being clustered around one central score.

Wilcoxon signed ranks test is a non-parametric statistical test which uses data at the ordinal level of measurement and tests for differences between two sets of related data.

Wilcoxon rank sum test is a non-parametric statistical test which uses data at the ordinal level of measurement and tests for differences between two sets of unrelated data. An alternative to the Mann–Whitney *U* test.

Ethical issues and how to deal with them

Psychological investigators are potentially interested in all aspects of human behaviour and conscious experience. However, for ethical reasons, some areas of human experience and behaviour may be beyond the reach of experiment, observation or other form of psychological investigation.

There are some basic questions you should ask yourself before you start collecting any data. These points of guidance come from the OCR specification, but will apply to all psychology investigations.

- **Should I be conducting this study at all?**
- **What is the most ethical way of carrying it out?**
- **Am I competent to undertake this study?**
- **Do I have the participants' informed consent to take part in my study?**
- **How do I ensure that all research records are confidential and anonymous?**
- **How do I ensure that my personal conduct is professional?**

In all circumstances you must consider the ethical implications and psychological consequences for the participants in your research. The essential principle is that the investigation should be considered from the standpoint of the participants and any foreseeable threats to their psychological well-being, health, values or dignity should be eliminated. It should be borne in mind that the best judge of whether an investigation will cause offence may be members of the population from which the participants in the research are to be drawn.

If your study has any of the following features, you should discuss these with your teacher/supervisor before proceeding any further with the study:

1 **using drugs or alcohol**
2 **interviews/recall of personal memories**
3 **unpleasant or loud auditory or visual stimuli**

4 prolonged exposure to auditory stimuli

5 tasks with a high failure rate

6 procedures likely to change participants' mood or stress them in any way

7 tasks which could threaten safety in any way

8 participants aged under 16 years or elderly participants

9 participants whose capacity to give consent may be in doubt

10 participants being investigated for a problem which has received medical, psychiatric, clinical psychological or other similar attention

11 participants recruited from special sources (e.g. prisons, hospitals)

12 participants being investigated in connection with a performance deficit

13 misleading participants about an experiment

14 withholding significant prior information

15 observing participants unawares, or analysing data the participants did not realise would be used by you for research purposes

16 participants with a mental handicap

17 deprivation or restriction (e.g. food or sleep)

18 any inducement for participants to take part (e.g. payment)

19 possible disclosure of confidential information (e.g. to other participants)

20 possible identification of participants (e.g. when reporting results)

21 procedures which might be harmful or distressing to people in a specially vulnerable state (e.g. depressed, anxious, bereaved, etc.)

22 procedures from which participants would not feel free to withdraw at any point

23 procedures affecting the participants' ability to give continuing consent, or to conduct themselves safely afterwards (e.g. alcohol use, hypnosis)

24 information-gathering on sensitive issues such as sexual, racial, religious or political attitudes

25 procedures where participants have little time to decide whether to participate (or continue)

26 procedures where participants might upset or harm one another

A B C D E F G H I J K L M N O P Q R S T U V W X Y Z

27 discussion or investigation of personal topics (e.g. relationships, feelings of success and failure) or any other procedure in which participants may have an emotional investment

28 lack of debriefing, or inclusion of information in debriefing that could upset or embarrass participants etc.

29 personality questionnaires or rating scales

30 any other reason(s) for possible ethical concern that you can think of.

Resolving ethical issues – the BPS ethical guidelines

In this section you will find advice on some of the major ethical issues you will come across in your research, and how to deal with them. If in doubt, however, you should check carefully with your teacher before proceeding.

CONSENT

BPS guidelines:

Whenever possible, the investigators should inform all participants of the objectives of the investigation. The investigators should inform the participants of all aspects of the research or intervention that might reasonably be expected to influence willingness to participate. Research with children or with participants who have impairments that limit understanding and/or communication such that they are unable to give their real consent requires special safeguarding procedures.

Unless you are observing people in public places, your participants should be volunteers, and therefore have the right to know exactly what they are letting themselves in for before they agree to take part. This does not mean telling them every minor detail of the study, but rather emphasising those aspects of the study that may influence their willingness to take part. The key factor in consent is that it should be informed.

Allowing your participants the opportunity to give their informed consent is a fundamentally important part of any investigation. It is worth investing a little time thinking how this can best be achieved. It is acceptable for this to be done verbally, with you providing them with any relevant information that might influence their decision to take part. However, it is more professional (and gives you and your teacher tangible evidence that you have handled this aspect of the investigation competently) if this is done in writing. The sample informed consent form on the next page gives you some idea of how you might construct your own form that is appropriate for your investigation.

BRAMPTON SIXTH FORM COLLEGE
DEPARTMENT OF PSYCHOLOGY

Name of Project: ....
....

You are invited to participate in a study of [*state what is being studied*]. The purpose of the study is [*state what the study is designed to discover or establish*].

The study is being conducted by [*provide the names of the Investigators, their BSFC affiliations, and contact telephone numbers*].

If you decide to participate, you will be asked to [*describe the tasks or procedures, their frequency and duration, and the information to be obtained. Acknowledge any recording using audiotapes, videotapes, or photographs. Describe any risks or discomforts. Describe any payment of money or other remuneration*].

Any information or personal details gathered in the course of the study are confidential. No individual will be identified in any publication of the results. [*Acknowledge who will have access to the data.*]

If you decide to participate, you are free to withdraw your consent and to discontinue participation at any time without having to give a reason and without consequence.

I, [*participant's name*] have read and understand the information above and any questions I have asked have been answered to my satisfaction. I agree to participate in this research, knowing that I can withdraw at any time without consequence. I have been given a copy of this form to keep.

Participant's Name: ....
Participant's Signature: ....
Date: ....

Investigator's Name: ....
Investigator's Signature: ....
Date: ....

A model for an informed consent form

WITHDRAWAL FROM THE INVESTIGATION

BPS guidelines:

At the onset of the investigation investigators should make plain to participants their right to withdraw from the research at any time, irrespective of whether or not payment or other inducement has been offered. In the light of experience of the investigation or as a result of debriefing, the participant has the right to withdraw retrospectively any consent given, and to require that their own data, including recordings, be destroyed.

If people agree to take part in your study, you must inform them that they can withdraw at any point. This also means they can also withdraw their data from the study (if they are particularly concerned about something that has happened) without any expressions of disappointment, disgust or any other negative feedback from the researcher. Because of the way in which some people regard their role as participants in an investigation, they may feel awkward about terminating their part in the study. This may happen, particularly if they are friends or relatives, or simply because they realise how important this study is to you. You should be sensitive to this possibility, and be prepared to stop the study if you sense your participant is becoming uncomfortable with their role. This is a sign of maturity and sensitivity on your part, so should not be looked upon as a failure in your role as researcher.

Some people, most notably children, may not be able to give their informed consent, therefore you should take special care when using them as participants, and seek the advice of your teacher before the study starts. As a general rule, when dealing with minors, you need the permission of a parent or other person acting in loco parentis. You should also decide whether consent from the child themselves is possible, as many children *will* understand what you are trying to do, and will be capable of deciding for themselves whether they want to take part.

DECEPTION

BPS guidelines:

The withholding of information or the misleading of participants is unacceptable if the participants are typically likely to show unease once debriefed. Where this is in any doubt, appropriate consultation must precede the investigation. Intentional deception of the participants over the purpose and general nature of the investigation should be avoided whenever possible.

It is quite unacceptable to trick people into participating in your study by deliberately misleading them about the true purpose of the study. This is a difficult one however, as it may well be the case that the study would not work if participants knew the real reason for your work. In such cases, you may introduce a 'cover story' so that participants do not try to adjust their behaviour to match their expectations of what you are looking for. Using a cover story may be acceptable provided it does not unduly influence participants' ability to give *informed* consent. There are a number of ways you can check this. First, you might take a small sample of participants and explain to them what you intend to do. Tell them about the deception and ask them if they would still have volunteered to take part had they known the true purpose of the study. Second, you might judge whether participants object to the deception during the debriefing at the end of every participant's contribution to the study.

DEBRIEFING

BPS guidelines:

In studies where the participants are aware that they have taken part in an investigation, when the data have been collected, the investigator should provide the participants with any necessary information to complete their understanding of the nature of the research. The investigator should discuss with the participants their experience of the research in order to monitor any unforeseen negative effects or misconceptions.

This is a post-experimental interview in which you endeavour to restore the participant to the same psychological state they were in when they entered your investigation. Sometimes it is seen as sufficient to inform the participant of the true nature and purpose of the experiment, and to answer any questions participants may have. You will, of course, be asked questions like 'How did I do?' and 'How does that compare to other people' so you should be prepared to answer these diplomatically. Do not say 'Absolutely dreadful ... you are clearly the worst I've had'. Nor should you say 'Fine, wonderful, best so far'. You should simply offer something more neutral such as 'You were fine, but I can't say more until I've done the analysis'. Debriefing is especially vital when participants have been deceived in any way during the experiment, and you should especially look out for any signs of irritation concerning the deception used. Remember, debriefing should be an important part of your investigation, so don't just say 'Cheers' and walk away.

CONFIDENTIALITY

BPS guidelines:

Subject to the requirements of legislation, information obtained about a participant during an investigation is confidential unless otherwise agreed in advance. Investigators who are put under pressure to disclose confidential information should draw this point to the attention of those exerting such pressure.

Any information you obtain from participants should be treated as confidential. You may not be able to guarantee complete confidentiality (your report, including this data, will be read by others, including your teacher), but you should be able to guarantee complete anonymity. This means taking steps to make identification of your participants virtually impossible. Never use their real names or give any other information by which they might be identified. You may need to keep individual records, so these should be kept in a safe place and destroyed *properly* once your coursework is complete.

PROTECTION OF PARTICIPANTS

BPS guidelines:

Investigators have a primary responsibility to protect participants from physical and mental harm during the investigation. Normally the risk of harm must be no greater than in ordinary life.

Although it seems obvious, it does need to be emphasised that participants must *always* be protected from any sort of harm during your investigation. There are many ways you can cause harm to participants, some physical (e.g. getting them to smoke, drink or drink coffee excessively) some psychological (e.g. making them feel inadequate, embarrassing them, etc.). Be aware of how your participants might feel during the study, and try to minimise any harmful experiences.

OBSERVATIONAL RESEARCH

BPS guidelines:

Studies based upon observation must respect the privacy and psychological well-being of the individuals studied. Unless those being observed give their consent to being observed, observational research is only acceptable in situations where those observed would expect to be observed by strangers.

If you decide to carry out field research, you must respect people's rights to privacy.

Of course, if you restrict your observations to behaviour that is clearly public, there should not be too much of a problem. People in public situations expect to be observed by others, and provided you take steps to preserve their anonymity, observation should not intrude upon their privacy. At the other extreme however, people may be 'spied' on in situations where they would clearly expect their behaviour not to be observed (for example, in their own homes, offices or changing rooms). Although the degree of privacy possible in these settings varies from time to time, there is still general agreement that these are areas where an invasion of privacy would be inappropriate. The following points might be used to determine where a particular piece of research lies on the privacy continuum, and therefore how acceptable observation is under such circumstances.

- **How public the setting is – people can less reasonably expect privacy in shopping malls or football grounds than in the private settings of their own homes.**

- **The degree of anonymity provided – privacy is maintained when the link between an individual and the information obtained is severed.**

- **The nature of the information disclosed – certain information (e.g. about sexual practices or criminal activities) is considered more sensitive and poses a greater risk to participants than does other information. You must exercise careful ethical judgement when dealing with such sensitive information as this may be seen as an invasion of privacy.**

Coursework report checklist

The following checklist can be used when reviewing your coursework report. It is based on the AQA (A) requirements for an experimental study, but careful scrutiny of the specific requirements for your specification (see Chapters 12–15), or for an investigation that is non-experimental, should make it possible for you to adapt this list for your own needs.

Project brief

Have you:
- [ ] stated your aim and hypotheses?
- [ ] explained why a directional or non-directional hypothesis has been used?
- [ ] identified your research method and design?
- [ ] explained why this research method/design has been used?
- [ ] identified possible sources of bias and confounding variables?
- [ ] stated how possible sources of bias and confounding variables have been dealt with?
- [ ] explained your minimum level of statistical significance?
- [ ] stated your strategy for dealing with any ethical issues?

Abstract

Have you stated:
- [ ] the topic area studied?
- [ ] the aim/hypothesis?
- [ ] brief details of the method used?
- [ ] the principal findings?
- [ ] the main implications of the findings?

Introduction, aims and hypotheses

Have you:
- ☐ stated the general area of your study?
- ☐ referred to relevant and carefully selected background studies?
- ☐ reported your reasons for studying this topic?
- ☐ clearly stated your aim(s)?
- ☐ precisely stated: (a) the alternative hypothesis(es) and (b) the null hypothesis(es)?
- ☐ stated whether the alternative hypotheses are directional or non-directional?
- ☐ reported how you arrived at these aims/hypotheses?
- ☐ organised your introduction in a logical way?

Method

Have you:
- ☐ divided this section into suitable subsections?

Have you stated:
- ☐ the design used?
- ☐ the nature of any experimental groups/conditions?
- ☐ the nature of any control groups/conditions?
- ☐ the IV and DV or the variables correlated?
- ☐ stated the minimum level of statistical significance you will accept?
- ☐ your number of participants?
- ☐ the population from which participants were drawn?
- ☐ how participants were selected/sampled?
- ☐ how participants were allocated to experimental groups/conditions?
- ☐ relevant characteristics of participants, e.g. age range, sex?
- ☐ details of all apparatus and materials used?

A
B
C
D
E
F
G
H
I
J
K
L
M
N
O
P
Q
R
S
T
U
V
W
X
Y
Z

☐ any standardised instructions given to participants?

☐ the procedure followed in such a way that someone else could replicate it precisely using your description?

Results

Have you:

☐ provided a summary table of results?

☐ provided titles for all graphs, charts and data tables?

☐ labelled all axes and columns of your graphs, charts and data tables?

☐ used appropriate descriptive/inferential statistical techniques?

☐ described any trends in your data?

☐ stated full reasons why a particular statistical test was selected to analyse your data?

☐ reported appropriately your observed and critical values?

☐ reported your level of statistical significance?

Discussion

Have you stated:

☐ the results that you obtained?

Have you discussed:

☐ what your results mean in terms of your aims/hypotheses?

☐ your findings with reference to the studies quoted in your introduction?

☐ the limitations of your study?

☐ how improvements could be made to the study if it were to be done again?

☐ suggestions for follow-up studies?

☐ any wider implications of your findings?

Conclusion

Have you: ☐ briefly summarised your main findings?

References

Have you: ☐ provided full references for all sources used and quoted by names?

☐ written references in a conventional style?

Appendices

Have you: ☐ provided copies of such things as stimulus materials and experimental layouts?

☐ provided a table of raw data?

☐ included specimen statistical calculations?

☐ provided appropriate titles and labelling for all appendices?

Presentation

Have you: ☐ written your report in a concise scientific style?

☐ structured your report logically into sections?

☐ avoided unnecessary repetition or irrelevancy?

☐ provided a contents page and numbered your pages?

☐ presented your report in such a way that some one else could precisely replicate the study from your description?

☐ linked all graphs, charts and data tables into your text?

☐ acknowledged all sources of help with your coursework?

[Source: Davies, G.D. (2001), in M. Cardwell, E. Clark and C. Meldrum *Psychology for A2 Level*. Collins Educational, 571–2. Reprinted with permission]

A B C D E F G H I J K L M N O P Q R S T U V W X Y Z

A–Z of coursework resources

1 Books

A number of texts have been specially written to provide ideas for psychology coursework. Two of these are:

Title and Author	Publisher	ISBN
Flanagan, C. (1998). *Practicals for Psychology: A Student Workbook.*	Routledge	0 416157749
McIlveen, R. et al. (1992). *BPS Manual of Psychology Practicals: Experiment, Observation and Correlation*	BPS	1 854330748

Some texts give you detailed knowledge about classic studies in psychology. You may be able to get some ideas from the experts. Most of these studies will be beyond the scope of a humble AS or A level project, but they may just sow the seeds of an idea.

Title and Author	Publisher	ISBN
Banyard, P. & Grayson, A. (2001). *Introducing Psychological Research: Seventy Studies that Shape Psychology* (2nd edition)	Palgrave	0 333912519
Gross, R.D. (1999). *Key Studies in Psychology* (3rd edition)	Hodder & Stoughton	0 34072045X

2 Useful internet sites

Psychological Research on the Net – American Psychological Society

http://psych.hanover.edu/APS/exponnet.html

Posted by the American Psychological Society, this website presents an extensive annotated list of psychological research currently being conducted on the Web. Topics include health psychology, personality studies, psychology and religion, sensation and perception, social psychology, neural psychology, clinical psychology, developmental psychology, cognition, emotions and others. Links are provided to the listed websites. You may actually want to take part in some of these studies, or look at what other people are doing by way of inspiration for your own research.

Internet psychologist

Internet psychologist contains a huge list of links to many psychology sites. The index is at:

http://www.sosig.ac.uk/vts/psychologist/index.htm

If you're a beginner, this site contains a good tutorial on internet information skills for psychologists. Another link in internet psychologist is 'Web-Lab'. Once you have opened this one, scroll to the bottom of the page and click 'To the lab'. If you're feeling like a challenge, you could try some of the on-line experiments. You might find some good ideas for you own research here.

Psychological Science on the net

http://www.psychologicalscience.net/

Try 'Psychology topics' then follow the link to 'Research Methods'. This will take you to all the different psychological topics covered by the site. Choose the broad area of your chosen topic (e.g. comparative or social) and then the next pages will open up all the relevant links in that area.

Bill Trochim's site

http://trochim.human.cornell.edu/

This will get you to Bill Trochim's Center for Social Research Methods. Here you will find a rich source of information on all kinds of research methods, both quantitative and qualitative. Click on 'Knowledge Base' and then 'Content'. You will need to select from the huge list of headings that appears as this site contains some very advanced topics. Use your Specification to help you find what you need, e.g. there are (lengthy but good) sections on interviewing and scaling procedures for questionnaires.

PsychExperiments

http://psychexps.olemiss.edu/

PsychExperiments is an on-line cognitive and social psychology laboratory site that has been developed with funding from the US Department of Education. The site consists of a set of interactive experiments, a data archive, download utilities for both data and experiments, downloadable Excel macros for analysing data from the experiments, and support materials for those who want to use and/or develop experiments at the site.

PSYCLINE

http://www.psycline.org/journals/psycline.html

PSYCLINE'S Article Locator gives you an easy-to-use interface to article databases on the Web. This is an ideal way to browse through journal article abstracts relating to your research project. You will need to be patient when looking through journals by publisher but it is worth the effort. Not everything is covered but it is an excellent resource nonetheless when carrying out your initial reading around the area of your research interest.

Other sites with links

Two other sites provide huge numbers of links:

http://links2go.net/more/spsp.clarion.edu/mm/RDE3/start/

http://methods.fullerton.edu/noframesindex.html

These can be especially good for finding research-related topics such as discussions of ethical issues, qualitative and quantitative debates and the role of science in psychology as well as some of the more usual research methods and statistics. The second site has pages that look like the contents of a text-book. Clicking on these sends you off to other links, e.g. through 'ethics' you can find links to discussions of controversial experiments.

The Association for the Study of Animal Behaviour

http://www.asab.org/

The ASAB is committed to increasing awareness about animal behaviour in schools and colleges. If your interest in psychology centres more around the study of non-humans, there are a number of practicals that would be acceptable given the specific ethical constraints on animal research for pre-university students. The ASAB website contains samples of these, or you can get hold of a copy of the following text from the ASAB Education Officer, Michael Dockery.

Animal Behaviour: Practical Work and Data Response Exercises for Sixth Form Students by Michael Reiss and Michael Dockery.
This book has been designed to meet the requirements of teachers (and students) of A level Biology, Human Biology, Social Biology and Psychology. It consists of practicals, suggestions for projects and data response exercises, together with sections on carrying out observational and experimental studies, the statistical treatment of data, useful references and suppliers of livestock and equipment.
The book costs £4 (including packing and postage). It is available from:
    Michael Dockery

ASAB Education Officer
Department of Biological Sciences
John Dalton Building
Manchester Metropolitan University
Chester Street
Manchester
M1 5GD
UK
tel: 0161-247-1149
fax: 0161-247-6365
email: m.dockery@mmu.ac.uk

S-cool

http://www.s-cool.co.uk/

An online revision site that covers AS and A level Psychology. An excellent resource to fine-tune your research skills, or in fact any other area of your AS and A level Psychology specification.

British Psychological Society (BPS)

This authoritative site contains much useful information including access to the latest version of the BPS ethical guidelines.

www.bps.org.uk

or they can be contacted at:
British Psychological Society
St. Andrews House
48 Princess Rd East
Leicester
LE1 7DR

A
B
C
D
E
F
G
H
I
J
K
L
M
N
O
P
Q
R
S
T
U
V
W
X
Y
Z

3 Magazines

Magazine	Details
Psychology Review www.philipallan.co.uk	A quarterly magazine which is highly suitable for AS and A level Psychology students, and which contains articles and features (including coursework) on topics from all four psychology specifications. Clearly presented information and highly useable for students at this level. Published by: Philip Allan Updates Market Place Deddington Oxfordshire OX15 0SE
Psychology Today	Articles, news and research reports from the field of psychology. Published monthly, overseas subscription is currently \$30 per year. PO Box 51844 Boulder Colorado 80323-1844 US

Statistical tables

Table A1 Critical values of T in the Wilcoxon Signed Ranks Test

	Levels of significance			
	One-tailed test			
	0.05	0.025	0.01	0.001
	Two-tailed test			
	0.1	0.05	0.02	0.002
Sample size				
$N = $ 5	$T \leq 0$			
6	2	0		
7	3	2	0	
8	5	3	1	
9	8	5	3	
10	11	8	5	0
11	13	10	7	1
12	17	13	9	2
13	21	17	12	4
14	25	21	15	6
15	30	25	19	8
16	35	29	23	11
17	41	34	27	14
18	47	40	32	18
19	53	46	37	21
20	60	52	43	26
21	67	58	49	30
22	75	65	55	35
23	83	73	62	40
24	91	81	69	45
25	100	89	76	51
26	110	98	84	58
27	119	107	92	64
28	130	116	101	71
29	141	125	111	78
30	151	137	120	86
31	163	147	130	94
32	175	159	140	103
33	187	170	151	112

Calculated T must be EQUAL TO or LESS THAN the table (critical) value for
significance at the level shown.

SOURCE: Adapted from R. Meddis, *Statistical Handbook for Non-Statisticians*, McGraw-Hill, London (1975).

A
B
C
D
E
F
G
H
I
J
K
L
M
N
O
P
Q
R
S
T
U
V
W
X
Y
Z

Table A2a Critical values of U for a one-tailed test at 0.025; two-tailed test at 0.05* (Mann–Whitney)

n_2 \ n_1	1	2	3	4	5	6	7	8	9	10	11	12	13	14	15	16	17	18	19	20
1	—	—	—	—	—	—	—	—	—	—	—	—	—	—	—	—	—	—	—	—
2	—	—	—	—	—	—	—	0	0	0	0	1	1	1	1	1	2	2	2	2
3	—	—	—	—	0	1	1	2	2	3	3	4	4	5	5	6	6	7	7	8
4	—	—	—	0	1	2	3	4	4	5	6	7	8	9	10	11	11	12	13	13
5	—	—	0	1	2	3	5	6	7	8	9	11	12	13	14	15	17	18	19	20
6	—	—	1	2	3	5	6	8	10	11	13	14	16	17	19	21	22	24	25	27
7	—	—	1	3	5	6	8	10	12	14	16	18	20	22	24	26	28	30	32	34
8	—	0	2	4	6	8	10	13	15	17	19	22	24	26	29	31	34	36	38	41
9	—	0	2	4	7	10	12	15	17	20	23	26	28	31	34	37	39	42	45	48
10	—	0	3	5	8	11	14	17	20	23	26	29	33	36	39	42	45	48	52	55
11	—	0	3	6	9	13	16	19	23	26	30	33	37	40	44	47	51	55	58	62
12	—	1	4	7	11	14	18	22	26	29	33	37	41	45	49	53	57	61	65	69
13	—	1	4	8	12	16	20	24	28	33	37	41	45	50	54	59	63	67	72	76
14	—	1	5	9	13	17	22	26	31	36	40	45	50	55	59	64	67	74	78	83
15	—	1	5	10	14	19	24	29	34	39	44	49	54	59	64	70	75	80	85	90
16	—	1	6	11	15	21	26	31	37	42	47	53	59	64	70	75	81	86	92	98
17	—	2	6	11	17	22	28	34	39	45	51	57	63	67	75	81	87	93	99	105
18	—	2	7	12	18	24	30	36	42	48	55	61	67	74	80	86	93	99	106	112
19	—	2	7	13	19	25	32	38	45	52	58	65	72	78	85	92	99	106	113	119
20	—	2	8	13	20	27	34	41	48	55	62	69	76	83	90	98	105	112	119	127

* Dashes in the body of the table indicate that no decision is possible at the stated level of significance. For any n_1 and n_2 the observed value of U is significant at a given level of significance if it is equal to or less than the critical values shown.

SOURCE: R. Runyon and A. Haber (1976) *Fundamentals of Behavioural Statistics* (3rd ed.) Reading, Mass.: McGraw-Hill, Inc.

Table A2b Critical values of U for a one-tailed test at 0.05; two-tailed test at 0.10* (Mann–Whitney)

n_2 \ n_1	1	2	3	4	5	6	7	8	9	10	11	12	13	14	15	16	17	18	19	20
1	–	–	–	–	–	–	–	–	–	–	–	–	–	–	–	–	–	–	0	0
2	–	–	–	–	0	0	0	1	1	1	1	2	2	2	3	3	3	4	4	4
3	–	–	0	0	1	2	2	3	3	4	5	5	6	7	7	8	9	9	10	11
4	–	–	0	1	2	3	4	5	6	7	8	9	10	11	12	14	15	16	17	18
5	–	0	1	2	4	5	6	8	9	11	12	13	15	16	18	19	20	22	23	25
6	–	0	2	3	5	7	8	10	12	14	16	17	19	21	23	25	26	28	30	32
7	–	0	2	4	6	8	11	13	15	17	19	21	24	26	28	30	33	35	37	39
8	–	1	3	5	8	10	13	15	18	20	23	26	28	31	33	36	39	41	44	47
9	–	1	3	6	9	12	15	18	21	24	27	30	33	36	39	42	45	48	51	54
10	–	1	4	7	11	14	17	20	24	27	31	34	37	41	44	48	51	55	58	62
11	–	1	5	8	12	16	19	23	27	31	34	38	42	46	50	54	57	61	65	69
12	–	2	5	9	13	17	21	26	30	34	38	42	47	51	55	60	64	68	72	77
13	–	2	6	10	15	19	24	28	33	37	42	47	51	56	61	65	70	75	80	84
14	–	2	7	11	16	21	26	31	36	41	46	51	56	61	66	71	77	82	87	92
15	–	3	7	12	18	23	28	33	39	44	50	55	61	66	72	77	83	88	94	100
16	–	3	8	14	19	25	30	36	42	48	54	60	65	71	77	83	89	95	101	107
17	–	3	9	15	20	26	33	39	45	51	57	64	70	77	83	89	96	102	109	115
18	–	4	9	16	22	28	35	41	48	55	61	68	75	82	88	95	102	109	116	123
19	0	4	10	17	23	30	37	44	51	58	65	72	80	87	94	101	109	116	123	130
20	0	4	11	18	25	32	39	47	54	62	69	77	84	92	100	107	115	123	130	138

* Dashes in the body of the table indicate that no decision is possible at the stated level of significance.
For any n_1 and n_2 the observed value of U is significant at a given level of significance if it is equal to or less than the critical values shown.

SOURCE: R. Runyon and A. Haber (1976) *Fundamentals of Behavioural Statistics* (3rd ed.) Reading, Mass.: McGraw-Hill, Inc.

Table A3 Critical values of χ^2

df	Level of significance for a one tailed-test					
	0.10	0.05	0.025	0.01	0.005	0.0005
	Level of significance for a two-tailed test					
	0.20	0.10	0.05	0.02	0.01	0.001
1	1.64	2.71	3.84	5.41	6.64	10.83
2	3.22	4.60	5.99	7.82	9.21	13.82
3	4.64	6.25	7.82	9.84	11.34	16.27
4	5.99	7.78	9.49	11.67	13.28	18.46
5	7.29	9.24	11.07	13.39	15.09	20.52
6	8.56	10.64	12.59	15.03	16.81	22.46
7	9.80	12.02	14.07	16.62	18.48	24.32
8	11.03	13.36	15.51	18.17	20.09	26.12
9	12.24	14.68	16.92	19.68	21.67	27.88
10	13.44	15.99	18.31	21.16	23.21	29.59
11	14.63	17.28	19.68	22.62	24.72	31.26
12	15.81	18.55	21.03	24.05	26.22	32.91
13	16.98	19.81	22.36	25.47	27.69	34.53
14	18.15	21.06	23.68	26.87	29.14	36.12
15	19.31	22.31	25.00	28.26	30.58	37.70
16	20.46	23.54	26.30	29.63	32.00	39.29
17	21.62	24.77	27.59	31.00	33.41	40.75
18	22.76	25.99	28.87	32.35	34.80	42.31
19	23.90	27.20	30.14	33.69	36.19	43.82
20	25.04	28.41	31.41	35.02	37.57	45.32
21	26.17	29.62	32.67	36.34	38.93	46.80
22	27.30	30.81	33.92	37.66	40.29	48.27
23	28.43	32.01	35.17	38.97	41.64	49.73
24	29.55	33.20	36.42	40.27	42.98	51.18
25	30.68	34.38	37.65	41.57	44.31	52.62
26	31.80	35.56	38.88	42.86	45.64	54.05
27	32.91	36.74	40.11	44.14	46.96	55.48
28	34.03	37.92	41.34	45.42	48.28	56.89
29	35.14	39.09	42.69	49.69	49.59	58.30
30	36.25	40.26	43.77	47.96	50.89	59.70
32	38.47	42.59	46.19	50.49	53.49	62.49
34	40.68	44.90	48.60	53.00	56.06	65.25
36	42.88	47.21	51.00	55.49	58.62	67.99
38	45.08	49.51	53.38	57.97	61.16	70.70
40	47.27	51.81	55.76	60.44	63.69	73.40
44	51.64	56.37	60.48	65.34	68.71	78.75
48	55.99	60.91	65.17	70.20	73.68	84.04
52	60.33	65.42	69.83	75.02	78.62	89.27
56	64.66	69.92	74.47	79.82	83.51	94.46
60	68.97	74.40	79.08	84.58	88.38	99.61

Calculated value of χ^2 must EQUAL or EXCEED the table (critical) values for significance at the level shown.

Abridged from R. A. Fisher and F. Yates, *Statistical Tables for Biological, Agricultural and Medical Research* (6th ed.) Longman Group UK Ltd (1974).

Table A4 Critical values of t

Degrees of freedom	Level of significance for a one-tailed test			
	0.05	0.025	0.01	0.005
	Level of significance for a two-tailed test			
	0.10	0.05	0.02	0.01
1	6.314	12.706	31.821	63.657
2	2.920	4.303	6.965	9.925
3	2.353	3.182	4.541	5.841
4	2.132	2.776	3.747	4.604
5	2.015	2.571	3.365	4.032
6	1.943	2.447	3.143	3.707
7	1.895	2.365	2.998	3.499
8	1.860	2.306	2.896	3.355
9	1.833	2.262	2.821	3.250
10	1.812	2.228	2.764	3.169
11	1.796	2.201	2.718	3.106
12	1.782	2.179	2.681	3.055
13	1.771	2.160	2.650	3.012
14	1.761	2.145	2.624	2.977
15	1.753	2.131	2.602	2.947
16	1.746	2.120	2.583	2.921
17	1.740	2.110	2.567	2.898
18	1.734	2.101	2.552	2.878
19	1.729	2.093	2.539	2.861
20	1.725	2.086	2.528	2.845
21	1.721	2.080	2.518	2.831
22	1.717	2.074	2.508	2.819
23	1.714	2.069	2.500	2.807
24	1.711	2.064	2.492	2.797
25	1.708	2.060	2.485	2.787
26	1.706	2.056	2.479	2.779
27	1.703	2.052	2.473	2.771
28	1.701	2.048	2.467	2.763
29	1.699	2.045	2.462	2.756
30	1.697	2.042	2.457	2.750
40	1.684	2.021	2.423	2.704
60	1.671	2.000	2.390	2.660
120	1.658	1.980	2.358	2.617
•	1.645	1.960	2.326	2.576

Calculated t must EQUAL OR EXCEED the table (critical) value for significance at the level shown.
SOURCE: Abridged from R.A. Fisher and F. Yates, *Statistical Tables for Biological Agricultural and Medical Research* (6th ed.) Longman Group UK Ltd (1974).

A B C D E F G H I J K L M N O P Q R S T U V W X Y Z

Table A5 Critical values of Spearman's rho (r_s)

		Level of significance for a one-tailed test		
		0.05	0.025	0.01	0.005
		Level of significance for a two-tailed test		
		0.10	0.05	0.02	0.01
$n =$	4	1.000			
	5	0.900	1.000	1.000	
	6	0.829	0.886	0.943	1.000
	7	0.714	0.786	0.893	0.929
	8	0.643	0.738	0.833	0.881
	9	0.600	0.700	0.783	0.833
	10	0.564	0.648	0.745	0.794
	11	0.536	0.618	0.709	0.755
	12	0.503	0.587	0.671	0.727
	13	0.484	0.560	0.648	0.703
	14	0.464	0.538	0.622	0.675
	15	0.443	0.521	0.604	0.654
	16	0.429	0.503	0.582	0.635
	17	0.414	0.485	0.566	0.615
	18	0.401	0.472	0.550	0.600
	19	0.391	0.460	0.535	0.584
	20	0.380	0.447	0.520	0.570
	21	0.370	0.435	0.508	0.556
	22	0.361	0.425	0.496	0.544
	23	0.353	0.415	0.486	0.532
	24	0.344	0.406	0.476	0.521
	25	0.337	0.398	0.466	0.511
	26	0.331	0.390	0.457	0.501
	27	0.324	0.382	0.448	0.491
	28	0.317	0.375	0.440	0.483
	29	0.312	0.368	0.433	0.475
	30	0.306	0.362	0.425	0.467

For $n > 30$, the significance of r_s can be tested by using the formula:

$$t = r_s \sqrt{\left(\frac{n-2}{1-r_s^2}\right)} \quad df = n-2$$

and checking the value of t in Table A4.

Calculated r_s must EQUAL or EXCEED the table (critical) value for significance at the level shown.

Table A6 Critical values of Pearson's *r*

	Level of significance for a one-tailed test			
	0.05	0.025	0.005	0.0005
df	Level of significance for a two-tailed test			
(*N* − 2)	0.10	0.05	0.01	0.001
2	0.9000	0.9500	0.9900	0.9999
3	0.805	0.878	0.9587	0.9911
4	0.729	0.811	0.9172	0.9741
5	0.669	0.754	0.875	0.9509
6	0.621	0.707	0.834	0.9241
7	0.582	0.666	0.798	0.898
8	0.549	0.632	0.765	0.872
9	0.521	0.602	0.735	0.847
10	0.497	0.576	0.708	0.823
11	0.476	0.553	0.684	0.801
12	0.475	0.532	0.661	0.780
13	0.441	0.514	0.641	0.760
14	0.426	0.497	0.623	0.742
15	0.412	0.482	0.606	0.725
16	0.400	0.468	0.590	0.708
17	0.389	0.456	0.575	0.693
18	0.378	0.444	0.561	0.679
19	0.369	0.433	0.549	0.665
20	0.360	0.423	0.537	0.652
25	0.323	0.381	0.487	0.597
30	0.296	0.349	0.449	0.554
35	0.275	0.325	0.418	0.519
40	0.257	0.304	0.393	0.490
45	0.243	0.288	0.372	0.465
50	0.231	0.273	0.354	0.443
60	0.211	0.250	0.325	0.408
70	0.195	0.232	0.302	0.380
80	0.183	0.217	0.283	0.357
90	0.173	0.205	0.267	0.338
100	0.164	0.195	0.254	0.321

Calculated *r* must EQUAL or EXCEED the table (critical) value for significance at the level shown.

SOURCE: F.C. Powell, *Cambridge Mathematical and Statistical Tables*, Cambridge University Press (1976). With kind permission of the publishers.

A B C D E F G H I J K L M N O P Q R S T U V W X Y Z

Table A7 Random numbers

03 47 43 73 86	39 96 47 36 61	46 98 63 71 62	33 26 16 80 45	60 11 14 10 95
97 74 24 67 62	42 81 14 57 20	42 53 32 37 32	27 07 36 07 51	24 51 79 89 73
16 76 62 27 66	56 50 26 71 07	32 90 79 78 53	13 55 38 58 59	88 97 54 14 10
12 56 85 99 26	96 96 68 27 31	05 03 72 93 15	57 12 10 14 21	88 26 49 81 76
55 59 56 35 64	38 54 82 46 22	31 62 43 09 90	06 18 44 32 53	23 83 01 30 30
16 22 77 94 39	49 54 43 54 82	17 37 93 23 78	87 35 20 96 43	84 26 34 91 64
84 42 17 53 31	57 24 55 06 88	77 04 74 47 67	21 76 33 50 25	83 92 12 06 76
63 01 63 78 59	16 95 55 67 19	98 10 50 71 75	12 86 73 58 07	44 39 52 38 79
33 21 12 34 29	78 64 56 07 82	52 42 07 44 38	15 51 00 13 42	99 66 02 79 54
57 60 86 32 44	09 47 27 96 54	49 17 46 09 62	90 52 84 77 27	08 02 73 43 28
18 18 07 92 46	44 17 16 58 09	79 83 86 16 62	06 76 50 03 10	55 23 64 05 05
26 62 38 97 75	84 16 07 44 99	83 11 46 32 24	20 14 85 88 45	10 93 72 88 71
23 42 40 64 74	82 97 77 77 81	07 45 32 14 08	32 98 94 07 72	93 85 79 10 75
52 36 28 19 95	50 92 26 11 97	00 56 76 31 38	80 22 02 53 53	86 60 42 04 53
37 85 94 35 12	83 39 50 08 30	42 34 07 96 88	54 42 06 87 98	35 85 29 48 38
70 29 17 12 13	40 33 20 38 26	13 89 51 03 74	17 76 37 13 04	07 74 21 19 30
56 62 18 37 35	96 83 50 87 75	97 12 25 93 47	70 33 24 03 54	97 77 46 44 80
99 49 57 22 77	88 42 95 45 72	16 64 36 16 00	04 43 18 66 79	94 77 24 21 90
16 08 15 04 72	33 27 14 34 90	45 59 34 68 49	12 72 07 34 45	99 27 72 95 14
31 16 93 32 43	50 27 89 87 19	20 15 37 00 49	52 85 66 60 44	38 68 88 11 80
68 34 30 13 70	55 74 30 77 40	44 22 78 84 26	04 33 46 09 52	68 07 97 06 57
74 57 25 65 76	59 29 97 68 60	71 91 38 67 54	13 58 18 24 76	15 54 55 95 52
27 42 37 86 53	48 55 90 65 72	96 57 69 36 10	96 46 92 42 45	97 60 49 04 91
00 39 68 29 61	66 37 32 20 30	77 84 57 03 29	10 45 65 04 26	11 04 96 67 24
29 94 98 94 24	68 49 69 10 82	53 75 91 93 30	34 25 20 57 27	40 48 73 51 92
16 90 82 66 59	83 62 64 11 12	67 19 00 71 74	60 47 21 29 68	02 02 37 03 31
11 27 94 75 06	06 09 19 74 66	02 94 37 34 02	76 70 90 30 86	38 45 94 30 38
35 24 10 16 20	33 32 51 26 38	79 78 45 04 91	16 92 53 56 16	02 75 50 95 98
38 23 16 86 38	42 38 97 01 50	87 75 66 81 41	40 01 74 91 62	48 51 84 08 32
31 96 25 91 47	96 44 33 49 13	34 86 82 53 91	00 52 43 48 85	27 55 26 89 62
66 67 40 67 14	64 05 71 95 86	11 05 65 09 68	76 83 20 37 90	57 16 00 11 66
14 90 84 45 11	75 73 88 05 90	52 27 41 14 86	22 98 12 22 08	07 52 74 95 80
68 05 51 18 00	33 96 02 75 19	07 60 62 93 55	59 33 82 43 90	49 37 38 44 59
20 46 78 73 90	97 51 40 14 02	04 02 33 31 08	39 54 16 49 36	47 95 93 13 30
64 19 58 97 79	15 06 15 93 20	01 90 10 75 06	40 78 78 89 62	02 67 74 17 33
05 26 93 70 60	22 35 85 15 13	92 03 51 59 77	59 56 78 06 83	52 91 05 70 74
07 97 10 88 23	09 98 42 99 64	61 71 62 99 15	06 51 29 16 93	58 05 77 09 51
68 71 86 85 85	54 87 66 47 54	73 32 08 11 12	44 95 92 63 16	29 56 24 29 48
26 99 61 65 53	58 37 78 80 70	42 10 50 67 42	32 17 55 85 74	94 44 67 16 94
14 65 52 68 75	87 59 36 22 41	26 78 63 06 55	13 08 27 01 50	15 29 39 39 43